Betty Crocker's
GUIDE TO
Easy Entertaining

Copyright ©1959 by General Mills, Inc. Published by Wiley Publishing, Inc. No part of this book may be reprinted in any form or by any means, electronic or mechanical, without permission in writing from the Publisher. Betty Crocker is a registered trademark of General Mills, Inc.

ISBN: 978-0-470-38626-2   Manufactured in China
Facsimile Edition 2008   10 9 8 7 6 5 4 3 2 1

4100   3848   3/09

We're excited to bring you this treasured edition of *Betty Crocker's Guide to Easy Entertaining.* All the recipes are exactly as they appeared in the original 1959 cookbook, to reflect the heritage of American cooking and baking. Eating habits may have changed, but the fond memories of sharing the delicious recipes from this cookbook remain the same. Some ingredients and food safety concerns have changed over the years, so you will want to use today's ingredients and methods when making these recipes.

OTHER BETTY CROCKER COOK BOOKS for the busy homemaker, the new bride, the career girl, the hostess who entertains two or twenty—and even for children learning to cook—are listed below. Each contains scores of easy, tested recipes, as well as menu suggestions and time-saving tips. Each is beautifully illustrated with photographs and drawings in color.

BETTY CROCKER'S
DINNER FOR TWO COOK BOOK
$1.00

BETTY CROCKER'S
GOOD AND EASY COOK BOOK
$1.00

BETTY CROCKER'S
COOK BOOK FOR BOYS AND GIRLS
$1.00

BETTY CROCKER'S
PICTURE COOK BOOK
$3.75 and $4.95

Dear Party-giver,

Perhaps you are one of my many friends who has written asking about suggestions for special entertaining. Each week I receive a growing number of letters asking for help.

It was a letter from someone I think of as a friend, though I have never met her, that started me on this collection of my replies to those requests.

"If you answered all of the questions I would like to ask you about how you entertain, you'd have to write a book," she wrote. "And I wish you would— a book about all of the details of good taste in the giving of parties as well as about the good taste of party foods."

So, here is a book about hospitality and how it can be easy and fun for the hostess as well as the guest.

In it are many of my own favorite party recipes, as well as anecdotes telling how my friends planned parties around specialties of their own.

I hope you will enjoy them as much as I enjoy happy memories of the good times they bring back to me.

Cordially,

Betty Crocker

Contents

INTRODUCTION	6
Planning Your Party	8
Invitations, Acceptances, and Regrets	15
When Guests Arrive	27
When Guests Leave	31
Dinners	41
Small Dinners	53
After Dinner Coffee	73
Buffet Dinners	78
Pot Luck Dinners	101
Come By for Dessert and Coffee	106
Midnight Suppers	109
Stag Parties	116
Lunches	120
Teas	132
Brunch	154
Barbecues	159
House Parties	167
INDEX	173

Introduction

THE LIVES of all of us have changed vastly since we watched our parents preparing for the first big party we can remember.

This is true of the brides as well as of the grandmothers among my readers.

Almost without exception, our houses are smaller than those of our parents. Our clothes and manners are far more casual. And our entertaining is less formal, because most of us now care for our homes with little or no help.

On the other hand, most of us are entertaining more often than we did in the past—if we are keeping up with the times.

The five-day week is now standard in virtually all industries.

Men have more time for fun and friends. So have women, even though so many are holding jobs as well as running their homes.

Big modern refrigerators, the great variety of frozen, canned, and convenience foods, and the new sensible approach to entertaining make hospitality easier than ever for those who plan parties in the modern way.

The dictionary defines hospitality as "being disposed to entertain with generous kindness."

This book is about each word in that definition:

How to be "disposed" by being ready in detail and in spirit.

How to "entertain" yourself as well as others.

How to be "generous" by providing delicious and suitable food.

How to serve it "with kindness" so that guests are not dismayed by a do-it-herself hostess who deserts them for her kitchen.

Planning Your Party

THE FIRST STEP, and a very important one, is deciding what kind of a party you can give most gracefully with the equipment, time, space, help, and money at your disposal.

A buffet for twenty is more fun for everyone than an attempt at a sit-down dinner for ten in a small space, if the hostess is her own cook and maid.

"The best way to keep up with the Joneses is not to try," one of my friends said recently to her young married daughter. She was in a panic about entertaining her husband's boss in their small apartment after going to several formal dinners at his big house. "Don't hire a maid for one evening in an attempt to equal his style of entertaining. He knows you can't afford it. He and his wife gave you their best. Now you do the same. Ask them to one of those good Sunday suppers you plan so well in advance. Hospitality isn't a contest. It is sharing the best *you* have."

Two happy memories are of different parties given by a hostess who had learned this.

When I first met her, she had a big house, a cook, and a maid. Her dinner parties, though never stiff, might properly be described as formal. She usually asked ten or twelve guests. Appetizers were served in the living room. Three or four courses followed in the dining room. We returned to the living room for coffee.

I loved to go there. She had a talent for combining congenial people. There was lots of laughter, good talk, good food, and our hostess seemed so charming and calm as the separate courses were brought to her without flurry from the kitchen.

I remember reporting one of her parties to another friend in a glow of appreciation for the planning that made it seem to run so easily.

"Who couldn't do the same with two in the kitchen?" she answered rather crisply. "I'd like to see her serve twelve for dinner in a house with no dining room, a couple of grammar school kids under foot, no help—and no flurry!"

Recently I had a chance to see her do just that.

They had moved to a much smaller house. The table was in a dining area off the living room instead of in a dining room. It was set with the same shining silver and festive china when we arrived, but, instead of a first course at the table, canapés that did not need forks or plates were passed by her youngsters. They had had their supper and disappeared to watch television in their bedroom before we sat down to dinner.

We served ourselves with the main course dishes which were lined up on a long book shelf near the table. Instead of a roast that needed carving at the last minute, or a steak that called for split-second timing, there was a big platter of smothered chicken. It had been cooked almost to a turn in the afternoon and needed only to be heated over low heat while guests were arriving. A tempting casserole of rice, pimientos, and black olives; a salad of romaine, avocado, and artichoke hearts; and rolls in a bread warmer were also in place.

Our hostess left the table only once to remove the dinner plates to the kitchen two by two. On her return trips she brought back two desserts. (Since she was not a maid, she did not follow the rule that calls for removing one plate at a time from the right.)

It was not a formal dinner party in the strict sense, but the meal had the same graceful, easy overtone of formality as the earlier ones I remembered with such pleasure because our hostess was with us almost throughout to enjoy it.

Planning the Guest List

The basic ingredient of parties is people.

"I just ask everyone I know and mix well," is the formula of one of my friends who specializes in very large informal teas,

Worth remembering are the words of one of my friends to her daughter who was complaining about having to entertain one of her husband's friends she termed "a crashing bore."

"Try to see him as he sees himself. Treat him as if he were fascinating—and maybe you'll find that he has something."

brunches, and buffet dinners. "Get enough nice people together, and everyone will find old or new friends to enjoy. Then all you have to worry about is food that can be fixed in advance."

That is a good rule for big affairs of any kind. Smaller ones take much more careful planning of the guest list.

"How do you go about planning your good parties?" I asked another friend who is noted for getting the right people together.

"I don't usually have a guest of honor," she said. "But in my own mind I start with one couple as sort of secret guests of honor. I ask myself, 'Whom will *they* like? Who will enjoy *them* the most?' And everything seems to fall into place."

Her words reminded me of advice I heard long ago and have never forgotten.

A group of us were trying to define "party spirit" as it relates to a hostess.

"To me, the answer lies in the word *giving* a party," said a wise older woman. "The hostess who thinks of her party as a gift to her friends can't go wrong—a gift of people with whom they'll have fun—a gift of food they will enjoy—a gift of herself by having that food ready to serve without confusion—and a gift of confidence by letting them know what kind of a party is planned and how to dress for it."

Her last sentence is one I wish all hostesses would remember.

I always am grateful to the friend who says something such as, "I am wearing an afternoon dress because Julie is coming directly from her office and won't have time to change," or "We are going to be gay and dress up. I thought I'd wear that off-the-shoulder yellow print," or "Dress any way you like. Some of us are going to be all done up, and others won't."

Part of the shine of any party is dimmed for the one guest who is out of step by being underdressed. And it is a hardship, as well as an embarrassment to the guest who arrives in chiffon and fragile evening slippers to find herself at a corn roast on a sandy shore.

Parties Start the Day Before

One of the best compliments I ever heard paid a hostess was from a very young man to his aunt. He had spent most of his life in boarding schools and summer camps, and was not accustomed to helping with preparations for parties at home.

During his military service, he was stationed near his aunt's home. She declared it open house for him and his friends. Each week end she went to no little trouble to prepare the mountains of food the very young can demolish so easily, but, being a canny hostess, she did this well before he arrived from camp with his gang.

One of the best rules for a successful meal and a serene hostess is "Test any new recipe before trying it at a party." You'll want to check the number of servings, and vary the seasoning to suit your taste.

Don't be known as a one-menu cook! Keep a file of guests and the foods you served them so that you won't set forth exactly the same meal, no matter how delicious, three or four times in succession for the same friends.

One afternoon I heard him planning a party for a dozen boys and their dates.

"That's too many! It really is too much trouble for your aunt!" protested his girl, wiser in the challenges of entertaining than he.

"No it isn't—my aunt never goes to any trouble getting ready for a party, or giving one," he said happily.

His aunt gave me an amused smile.

"He'll learn, once he starts giving parties in his own home," she said. "But what could be nicer words to hear from any guest?"

I could not agree with her more heartily.

Even the smallest party involves many hours of planning, shopping, getting house and food ready—and cleaning up. The best ones are those that seem to be "no trouble." This effect can be achieved only by organizing every detail well in advance.

Before her first party in her new home, the mother of a bride I know gave her a present. It was a pad and pencil. "These are indispensable tools for any party," she said. "Using them means the difference between a success and a partial failure."

A carefully made shopping list is the only insurance against discovering at the last minute that some essential ingredient has been forgotten. Any party is off to a bad start if the host has to slip out the back door and rush to the grocery store at the last minute for an overlooked item, or if the hostess is frantically ironing napkins or guest towels when the first guests ring the bell.

So, the first rule is "Be ready"—table set, food to the point where it needs no attention for a while, ice cracked, cigarettes, matches, and ashtrays in place, and the various duties of your "staff" outlined and rehearsed, if possible.

Any but the tiniest children can be pressed into service in the first half hour of a party to the benefit of all concerned. At one house I love to visit, I am always greeted at the door by a smiling little eight-year-old who directs me to the room where I am to put wraps, leaving his mother and father free to remain in the living room to welcome each new arrival and make introductions. He is better than any butler.

Children love parties if they are allowed to participate. The important thing is to give them the responsibility of some clearly defined duty, and so let them learn about hospitality by sharing it. Also, a specific duty forestalls a child's almost irresistible impulse to show off when there are strangers in his home. The youngster who is allowed to help is almost automatically on his best behavior. They are much more apt to retire willingly when the time comes if they have shared a bit of the spotlight.

Invitations, Acceptances, and Regrets

"WHAT SHALL I do about this?" asked a young friend recently, handing me an undated note. It read:

> Darlings—can you join us next Saturday at 5:30?
>
> Lots to tell you. Also want you to meet our new neighbors, the Browns. You'll love them.
>
> Best—
>
> Ann

"I know *four* Anns!" she said. "There is no return address on the envelope to give me a hint. The postmark is smudged. We've been away for ten days, so I don't know when this arrived. Is 'next' Saturday last week or this one? Does 'darlings' mean my mother, who lives with us, as well as my husband? And does 5:30 mean an afternoon party or an early dinner?"

Her questions are a fine example of why the single most important rule about invitations is "Be specific."

Here are other questions that I hear most often:

When is the telephone best for invitations?

Nearly everyone I know uses the telephone for invitations with exception of the few times when notes are more convenient or sensible (or for the entirely formal events, such as a big wedding, that call for engraved invitations).

Telephoning an invitation is a pleasant and practical plan for two reasons: it gives the hostess a chance to run down her list in a short time, and if one friend has a prior engagement, reach out for another without delay; also, it is easier to be specific about all details in a brief chat.

For instance, a hostess might say, "I do hope you and Bob can come to dinner a week from Thursday. My sister and her husband will be here from Detroit. They love bridge, so I am hoping the Johnsons can come, too. That will give us two good tables after dinner at six-thirty."

These few words give the guest a clear picture of what is planned. A good answer would be, "We'd love to come. I'm sure we're free, but I'll check with Bob tonight to make sure he hasn't a business date, and call you tomorrow."

If the guest is uncertain about how to dress, if she can't get a baby sitter until 7, or if there is some diet problem to be discussed, such matters can be settled most easily and gracefully during a telephone talk.

What do you do about guests with special diet problems?

I admired the thoughtfulness of a hostess who was entertaining me for the first time, and who said, "By the way, I am so relieved that I found out in time that one of my other guests is forbidden to eat onions. It is so unkind to offer anything that is taboo. By any chance, are you allergic to sea food? I haven't decided, but I thought I'd make a new shrimp casserole recipe we brought back from Charleston."

I was able to assure her that anything she chose would please me, and I was sure it would because of the care she was putting into every aspect of her guests' comfort.

The thoughtful guest who is on such an extremely restricted diet as a salt-free one, for example, does best to regret an invitation to a meal. It is not kind to ask a hostess, who has her hands full anyway, to prepare an entirely separate meal for one. It is even more unkind to refuse the party dishes she has gone to such trouble to prepare. In this case it is better to say, "We are not dining out at all while Bob is on a limited diet, but we'd love to join you anytime you're planning an after-dinner party."

This gives the hostess a chance to say, "We'll miss you—but will you join us after dinner?" Or, if late-comers do not suit her plans, "I'm so sorry. We'll plan an evening together soon."

Jack Spratt could eat no fat, his wife could eat no lean

Should I mention the others I am inviting to a party?

It is not necessary to run through the whole guest list with each person invited. Other guests usually are mentioned for a reason, or to indicate what kind of a party is planned, such as, "I am asking everyone we know who is going to the PTA meeting to come back with us for coffee and cake," or when it is helpful to identify a newcomer to your group if confusion might otherwise result.

I remember one fairly absurd conversation I had with a Dr. Fellows who was seated beside me at dinner. We talked at cross purposes for ten minutes until it dawned on me, from something another guest said, that he held a doctorate in economics—not medicine. In such cases, it is easier for everyone if the hostess mentions in advance, "Dr. Werner is our new pastor, Dr. Rawson is head of the English Department, and Dr. Beech keeps us well."

When you are mixing up Democrats and Republicans who hold very passionate opinions, it is never amiss to say, "Joe is working hard on the election—and not for your candidate. But forgive him that, and you'll enjoy him."

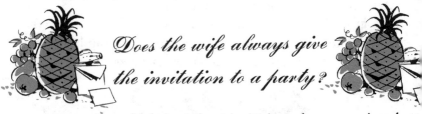

Does the wife always give the invitation to a party?

Except when a bachelor is host, invitations always are given by the hostess, or in her name, and are addressed to the other women involved, even if they have not met.

A good example is the way an invitation was given to me recently when I was in Cleveland for ten days. One of my business associates,

a man, asked if I were free to have dinner at his home during the week end. I said I would be delighted. He answered, "Fine. What's a good time for Marjorie to call you?" The next morning his wife, whom I had not met, was on the telephone to discuss the time most convenient for all of us, arrange to have another guest pick me up, and to suggest an informal dress since they planned a barbecue on the terrace. Because of the way she anticipated all of my questions, I was sure I was going to enjoy her hospitality, and I did.

If it is complicated for the hostess to reach a guest by telephone, and there is not time for a note, the invitation can be given by the host quite properly. He gives it in his wife's name, however, such as, "Betty has not been able to reach Jane, so she told me to ask you to save Friday night for us." In this case, the answer might be, "Jane *is* hard to reach. I'll ask her to call Betty in the morning."

How far in advance should I give an invitation?

There is no hard and fast rule about how far in advance invitations should be given. At least a week in advance of lunch or dinner is usual. Ten days to three weeks is safer, especially when you are planning to entertain a large group. Otherwise some of the friends you especially want may have made other plans for the time you have chosen.

A last-minute invitation calls for some explanation, however, such as "Bill came back from his fishing trip with a huge salmon— enough for ten! We are barbecuing it tomorrow night, and do hope you can join us at six." Or, "Just heard from the McKenzies. They are here for only two days, and are eager to see you. Can you come for lunch tomorrow?"

Without some explanation, guests may well think they were not part of your original plans. If this is actually the case, there is only one thing to do. Be frank. Say something like, "Can you help me out of a spot? Jane (or John) was coming to dinner tomorrow night, and was called out of town. Can you be an angel and fill in for me?"

When are written invitations best?

Written invitations are useful for friends who are hard to reach at home, and who find it inconvenient to take social calls at an office. Often, too, it is easier to write to a new acquaintance than to telephone.

Here, again, it is always the hostess who writes. The envelope is addressed to the wife only, never to "Mr. and Mrs. Jones," except in the case of an engraved invitation for the most formal of events.

Any kind of personal letter paper is used. Many people feel that a handwritten note is more attractive, but a typewritten one is entirely correct, though the signature is always handwritten, of course. Under any circumstances, don't forget to date the letter itself. Many people do not save envelopes when they open mail, and it is helpful to know when an invitation was written. A good sample is:

July 7

Dear Betty,

Jack and I hope you and Joe will come to brunch on Sunday, July 14, at 12:30, right after church. Bring the children. The youngsters are going to have a hot dog roast in the garden while the rest of us have a buffet on the porch.

Fondly,
Helen

For those you know slightly, a note might read:

Dear Mrs. Jones,

May 14

Bob and I so enjoyed our talk with you and Mr. Jones about Quebec. We hope you can come to dinner on Thursday, the 28th, at 7, and meet some friends who also know Canada well.

Yours truly,
Helen Conway Green
(Mrs. Robert W.)

14 Brook Terrace
City 8-3690

Invitations written on an engraved card, either a visiting card or a folded one, usually indicate a fairly large guest list. They are used most often for a tea, cocktail party, reception, or big buffet supper.

There is increasing use of the little printed cards, available at greeting card shops, with "Open House," "Shower," or "Party" printed on front, and with spaces for time, date, and place to be filled in under the fold. While very much less formal than invitations by note or personal card, I think they are an excellent idea —gay and also most practical. It is too easy to leave out some one essential detail (such as the date!) when writing a great many individual letters of invitation.

How are invitations to a child's party best given?

An invitation to a child's party never is given verbally to a child for the very sound reason that children forget or become easily confused about time and place.

Of course, children are going to talk with each other extensively about a party long before it happens, but an invitation is not official until the hostess-mother takes action, either verbally or by note. This may be her own letter to the mother of the young guest, or a written invitation which she obviously has sponsored—such as one of the printed cards mentioned above. This may be filled in by the child, or in the child's name. In this case, it is addressed to the young guest, and a written acceptance is addressed to the young host.

How soon must an invitation be answered?

Just as the first rule for invitations is "Be specific," so the first rule for answers is "Be prompt and definite."

An invitation should be accepted or refused within a day or two of the time received. It is an unkindness to delay for a week, leaving the hostess to wonder if her note was wrongly addressed and lost in the mail. And it is a dismaying thing for a hostess, planning a small Saturday night dinner, to hear, "We'd adore to come, but I won't know if we are going to the country until Thursday. May I let you know then?"

If you cannot say, "Yes," be merciful and say, "No," though it is entirely reasonable to feel your way in some such words as,

"We'd love to come, but we asked the Carters to have dinner with us on Saturday if they get back in time. So I'll have to refuse because I won't hear from them until Thursday."

This gives the hostess a chance to say, "I'm so sorry. I'll try you again soon," or "Do come if the Carters are delayed. I'll be hoping until the last minute you'll be with us."

Are invitations always answered in the way they are given?

Answers are usually made in the same form in which they were given, though there is much latitude in all informal invitations and acceptances. It is quite proper and usual to telephone an acceptance to a written invitation, though never to an office unless you are sure a social call over a business telephone is welcome. If the invitation is on a personal or a printed card, you may send your own engraved card back with "Happy to join you at 5:30 on May 15" written on it, but a telephoned answer, or a letter, is equally good practice.

The wife, who extends invitations, also answers them.

When an invitation is given to a couple, both are expected to refuse if one happens to be otherwise engaged, especially if that one is the husband. It is disconcerting to a hostess, who may be having her troubles finding enough men anyway, to hear, "Bill has a committee dinner that night— but I'd love to come."

Acceptances call for no more than some variant of "Yes," such as "Happy to join you," or "We'd love to come to your party," though it is a good idea to repeat time and date to make sure that there is no misunderstanding.

Refusing an invitation calls for a little more than a brief variant of "No," however—unless you want to imply that you never care to accept any invitation from that hostess.

A good form is something such as, "I am so very sorry. We're having dinner that night with Bill's parents—a family celebration. I couldn't be more disappointed at having to miss your party."

Must I always give a specific reason for refusing?

It is not necessary to explain in detail why you cannot accept an invitation, if you do not wish to do so, but it is important to regret in warmly cordial terms, such as, "We would love to accept, but we have another engagement. I do hope you will think of us again soon."

I am never flattered when a guest says, "I have another date, but maybe I can get out of it. I would so much rather come to your party. Let me try to escape and call you back."

This answer indicates to me that my acquaintance is socially unreliable, and I am inclined to be wary of her in the future. If she is willing to upset another friend's plan to indulge herself, the time may well come when she will upset mine!

An acceptance is a promise to appear. That promise should not be broken except for honest emergency such as illness or unexpected absence from town, no matter how much more attractive another and later invitation may be.

On the other hand, if your prior date is with friends who are rather likely to be on your hostess' list for a big party, also, it is only kind to her as well as to yourself to give her a hint in some such words as, "I'm so sorry we have a date. We have asked the Carters to go with us to the movies that night. . . ."

This gives your hostess a chance to say, "But I want the Carters, too! Let me call them and say I am breaking your date for the movies, and all of you come here."

It is easy to feel your way in much the same manner without putting your hostess in an embarrassing spot when you have a house guest you would like to bring by saying, "I'm so sorry we can't accept. My aunt is arriving that day for a short visit. Otherwise nothing would keep us away."

This gives the hostess a chance to say, "Of course you will want to be with her, but we'll miss you," if it does not suit her plans to add an extra woman. Or, "Will your aunt be too tired to come with you? I'd love to have her, too."

When Guests Arrive

THE PARTY IS officially under way with the first ring of the doorbell. Either host or hostess may open the door, and take wraps or direct the guest to the room where they are to be left. The important thing is for one or the other to keep an alert eye out for the new arrival, especially at a very large gathering, so that a stranger to the group is not left feeling lonesome and ignored on entering the living room.

At a very big party, each newcomer is introduced to several guests near at hand. The fact that everyone is under one roof is considered introduction to all of the others, though it is a good idea to make sure that those you particularly want to bring together are not left to find each other by chance.

In a small group, or early in a big party, each new arrival is introduced to the circle as a whole, "This is Mrs. Jones," or "Jane Jones," if first names are the custom among your friends. A couple need not be introduced separately. "Here are the Joneses," or "Jane and John Jones," or "Mr. and Mrs. Jones," are best if they join the party together. Each of the other guests is then introduced to the new arrival, going around the circle mentioning each name in turn, but certainly not repeating the name of the newcomer unless you think someone may have missed the initial introduction.

This is the one occasion where I think it is much more easy and sensible to modify the rule that men always must be introduced, or "presented," to women. It is cumbersome to introduce a newly arrived woman guest first to other women, and then back around the circle for introduction of the men to her. Of course, when introducing a guest to only two or three others, men are introduced to women, and the very much younger woman to an older one, according to the standard rule.

Men rise on being introduced to any woman, but the woman guest never rises unless she is being introduced to another woman very markedly her senior, or when a clergyman or other male guest of either great distinction or age is introduced to her. In a small group, all men rise when a woman enters the room for the first time. In a larger group, a man absorbed in a conversation need not rise until new arrivals draw near.

The good guest leaves his problems at the door, or certainly saves them for discussion later in the evening. The guest who bursts in with, "The most annoying thing happened last week! Let me tell you, and you say frankly if you think it was my fault . . ." and goes on with a long tale in the hallway is no help

Common sense is the best guide to the shaking of hands, or not. Guests being introduced across a room need bow only. The guest who is being introduced waits for the other to offer a hand. The easy, graceful gesture is always the best of manners.

to a hostess. Of course, she wants to hear all details of the misadventure, whatever it may be, but not at a moment when she should be paying attention to all of her guests, not to one only.

Barring some accident that requires first aid, such as a pin to secure a crucial button, the good guest demands the least possible attention from host and hostess immediately after arrival, and waits until things have simmered down before telling that long story, or asking that detailed question.

Bringing flowers to a hostess is a charming thought, but it is better to restrain that generous impulse unless you are sure of her needs. Too often, the unexpected gift of flowers can cause more pain than pleasure.

I saw a telling example of that recently. My hostess had spent the morning gathering branches of forsythia and banking them in great sprays that were enormously effective in her grey, white, and yellow rooms. Then in came a kind and generous young man bearing an armful of glowing red gladiolas. They were superb, but nothing could have been less welcome to my hostess at that moment.

"What on earth shall I put them in?" she whispered to me. "There isn't a vase bigger than a milk bottle not already in use. And *where* shall I put them? They shriek at the forsythia!"

Flowers brought to a party must be put in water immediately and proudly displayed in some prominent spot if the well-meaning guest's feelings are not to be hurt. So think twice about bringing a gift that may take your hostess out of circulation during one of her busiest times; don't make her rig a makeshift vase for lovely flowers which may be a false note in the decorations she has planned with much care.

On the other hand, if you have a garden in full bloom and your hostess does not have one, it is a delightful thing to say, "Let me bring you some of our lilacs. I can easily drop them by in the afternoon when I pick up the children." Or, if it is not convenient to deliver your bouquet early, suggest, "We can come ten minutes early with them if you like."

The guest who is delayed, and who will be much more than fifteen minutes late, should telephone the briefest report on the facts, such as, "We missed the ferry. This means we'll be forty-five minutes late. Please don't wait for us. We'll be along as soon as possible."

If someone other than the hostess answers the telephone it is best to leave the message, waste no more time in getting under way, and make your apologies and explanations after arrival.

The guest who arrives exactly on time has the blessing of any hostess, but better ten minutes late than ten minutes early! Nothing is more awkward for the hostess who has her time carefully planned than the arrival of early birds while she is making gravy, feeding children, or racing through her shower.

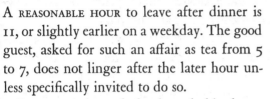

When Guests Leave

A REASONABLE HOUR to leave after dinner is 11, or slightly earlier on a weekday. The good guest, asked for such an affair as tea from 5 to 7, does not linger after the later hour unless specifically invited to do so.

Some member of the household always goes to the door with the departing guest. The guests who will be remembered gratefully are those who express thanks for a pleasant time and take themselves off without undue delay. Long chats in the hall or doorway, while other guests are wondering what has happened to host or hostess, are sure to take some of the shine off a party.

In an apartment house the host usually walks to the elevator with a departing guest, or stands in the doorway until the guest is safely in it.

In case a woman, particularly an elderly one, is leaving alone, he takes her to her car or a cab. If the street is dark and the bus or streetcar is several blocks away, or if transportation is in any way difficult for her, it is customary to make some special arrangement.

This is gracefully done by asking another guest, "Will it be convenient for you to give Mrs. Jones a lift? She is on your way."

No thanks other than those you give your host and hostess when leaving a party are a necessity, unless you have been a guest overnight. Then a "bread and butter note" always must be sent within a day or so.

However, nothing endears a friend to me more than a call or note after a party. It lifts the spirits of any hostess, faced with a house to return to order and a kitchen full of dishes, to hear a few kind words about her food, friends, and hospitality.

I wish young, unmarried men, especially, would do this more often. Many of them feel that, if they do call, they must be ready to give a return invitation, and so go off into silence leaving a hostess to wonder if her party was really the success she hoped for.

Of course, it is absurd for every guest at a very large party to telephone second thanks, but, after any moderately-sized gathering, a telephone call is welcome.

If it is not convenient to telephone, it is easy to dash off a note, "Still thinking about the good time I had with you—thanks again!"

Those few words warm the heart of any hostess, and are almost certain to bring another invitation soon.

Shrimp de Jonghe, p. 125 Prepare recipe ahead, divide into individual dishes. Just before serving, slip into preheated oven. Bake. Place in baskets as guests are seated. No last minute rush.

Midnight Supper

Remembrance Fruitcake, p. 112
Cheese Board, p. 111
Miniature Beefburgers

Emergency Meals

Beef stew is always a favorite. To a large can of beef stew add canned or leftover vegetables. Make dumplings using Bisquick (see package). Place on stew; cook over low heat 10 minutes uncovered, and 10 minutes covered.

Beef Stew
Tossed Green Salad
Crisp Bread Sticks
Chilled Canned Fruits
Macaroons

Flaming Chicken Brush drained canned whole chicken with mixture of ¼ cup butter, melted, and 2 tsp. gravy coloring. Sprinkle with black pepper. Heat in 400° oven 20 to 25 min. Heat small can of pitted black Bing cherries and can of Mandarin oranges. Drain fruit and place around chicken on serving plate. Brush chicken with 2 tsp. lemon extract and touch burning match to it.

Curried Shrimp Blend 1 can condensed cream of chicken soup with ¼ cup milk. Add 1 to 2 tsp. curry powder and two 5-oz. cans shrimp, drained and deveined. Heat thoroughly and serve over cooked rice tossed with chopped parsley and butter.

Buffet Supper

Baked Ham with
Washington Cherry Ham Glaze, p. 86
Baked Squash
Sauce for Baked Squash, p. 165
Hot Biscuits
Buttered Broccoli

Dinners

DINNER PARTIES, for a good reason, are the most popular form of home entertainment with nearly everyone.

They have a built-in party spirit because they come at the end of the day. Business is over. Now we are free to change to gayer clothes and to enjoy good food and companionship without having to hurry off to other duties or pleasures.

Big dinners, little dinners, barbecues, cookouts, cold dinners on a terrace, one-dish dinners on trays by a fire—there is some end-of-the-day meal suitable for every house and every budget.

Good food and good talk are enough entertainment in themselves. However, one of the most successful hostesses I know always has, in reserve, a plan for some game or activity when she is bringing strangers together and

◀ Baked Bean and Sausage Casserole, p. 87

Those who cannot recall any other tune nearly always can remember words of a high school theme song. After the stiffest newcomer has warbled, "Oh, Jefferson High School, I love you. You're like a sweetheart to me!" it is hard for him to feel like a stranger—or be treated as one.

is not sure that conversation will be as lively as she hopes.

"If my guests are enjoying each other's conversation, I never suggest a stunt or game," she says. "But it gives me confidence to have some diversion in mind in case things seem to be going slowly."

Music that all can join is a great "getter-together" of all ages. I remember with admiration one hostess who pulled a party out of the doldrums by turning the talk to old singing commercials. Soon everyone was eagerly trying to recall more of them than his neighbor.

Matching theme songs of old movies with their titles and stars is also a musical game all can play.

And old ballads and love songs are always popular, particularly if guests cooperate on a little close harmony.

A piano helps, but you don't have to have a musical instrument

for an impromptu musicale. One of the most memorable "orchestras" I ever heard was assembled in five minutes in her kitchen by a resourceful hostess who saw her party dying before her eyes. A tin wastebasket, coffee cans, and a breadbox became drums. Canisters of tea, glass jars of beans and rice made fine maracas of different tones. Pot-tops for percussion instruments and a wire whisk on a washboard completed her rhythm band, which was declared out of this world by its members as well as those who chose to dance to its tom-tom beat.

I have seen grown-ups have a joyous time with such children's games as *Three Thirds of a Ghost* and *I Went to the Forest,* but a wise hostess avoids any game that cannot be ended fairly quickly, or one in which everyone is not active most of the time. Boredom can grip a group quickly if the majority must sit silent while two or three stars act out a long, intricate charade.

Appetizers

"COME TO DINNER at seven," means that the hostess is planning to serve half an hour to forty-five minutes after that hour.

This does not mean that the guest is privileged to arrive at 7:30, however. The good guest turns up within a few minutes of the time specified for any party involving a meal, knowing that it takes a hostess about half an hour to welcome each guest, dispose of wraps, make introductions, serve appetizers, and get her dinner to the table.

Appetizers served before dinner are meant to whet the appetite, not to satisfy it. They are an introduction to a meal, rather than independent refreshment, and so should be planned to complement following courses. For instance, smoked oysters are not a happy choice before shrimp cocktail. A spread based on cream cheese is a good choice before a roast, but not before a creamed main dish.

Canapés, designed to be eaten grace-fully from the fingers, are savory little morsels of food—a base covered with a favorite topping. They can be served for refreshments, or with beverages in the living room to start a dinner off on a gay note.

Cold Appetizers

Since appetizers are the introduction to the whole meal, greatest care should be taken to make them especially attractive to the eye. However, no matter how beautiful, they are a failure if the cracker beneath the intricately decorated topping is limp and soggy. It is much wiser to offer one bowl of well-seasoned dip or spread surrounded by crisp crackers or toasted breadfingers than to hand around the most elaborate tidbits that have become spineless or crusty from long standing.

There are dozens of delicious and pretty canapés that can be assembled hours before your party, however, and that suffer not at all from storage in the refrigerator until needed.

Small cornucopias of ham, salami, cervelat, or dried beef, sliced very thin, filled with lightly seasoned cottage or cream cheese, and

Hors d'oeuvres are dainty finger foods, colorful and varied in size and shape, often exciting, too. Serve them on toothpicks stuck into a holder of wood, a grapefruit, apple, eggplant, pineapple, or bright red Edam cheese. Or serve hot ones from a chafing dish.

secured with a toothpick are festive looking and tasty. Ribbon sandwiches of white and brown breads, held together with a salty smooth spread, improve with several hours of chilling if well protected by foil or waxed paper.

One of my friends makes the most elaborate looking canapés with a pastry tube. She declares that they are put together far more quickly than the same ingredients spread by hand. They are so effective that I asked her for the recipe, and here it is.

GREEN LEAF CANAPÉS

Put one part of Bleu Cheese through a fine sieve (or mix it in a blender) and mix with three parts of cream cheese. Thin this mixture with a little cream, if necessary, and tint it pale green with food coloring. Pack it in a pastry bag or tube with a leaf point attached. Store in refrigerator.* Cut small squares of pumpernickel, rye, or close-grained white bread. Store them, well wrapped, in the refrigerator also. Fifteen minutes before guests are due, arrange the bread squares on a serving platter, and press a luscious green leaf of cheese on each. Add the tiniest of pearl onions or capers, if you wish.

*Remove and bring to room temperature before using.

"With the pastry tube, I can put together in five minutes what would take me twenty minutes to spread with a knife," she says. "And they really are especially pretty as well as good and easy."

There are many varieties of pastry-tube canapés worth exploring. Cream cheese flavored with anchovy paste, tinted pink, and pressed through a rosette point is an attractive contrast to the green leaves. Cream cheese in a ruffle around red caviar or spicy deviled ham gives variety to the tongue and to the eye.

One of the most festive looking canapé trays I know, and one of the easiest to assemble just before guests arrive is:

CANAPÉ CREAM PUFFS

In the morning, prepare and bake bite-sized cream puffs by following directions on the package of ready-mixed ingredients, using 1 level tsp. of dough for each puff. Each stick of Betty Crocker Cream Puff Mix makes about 60 of these miniatures. Let them cool. Split them with a sharp knife. Prepare fillings and set them aside also. If the fillings are not chilled, they go more quickly and smoothly into the crisp, delicately browned puffs. Any well-seasoned mixture that is not too moist is suitable, such as cream cheese or liver paté combined with minced onions or green olives. An especially good one is:

DEVILED CHEESE FILLING
FOR CREAM PUFFS

1 cup grated American cheese	½ tsp. Worcestershire sauce
¼ tsp. prepared mustard	1 tsp. grated onion
3 tbsp. mayonnaise	5 or 6 drops Tabasco sauce
	¼ tsp. celery seeds

Mix well. *Makes 1 cup.*

MUSHROOM CANAPÉS

Use raw unpeeled button mushroom caps. Cut a tiny slice from each cap so it will not roll. Fill with cream cheese seasoned with salt and curry powder. Top with a small sprig of parsley.

Four or five canapés for each guest is enough before a small dinner. When I am serving a small group, I usually offer just one kind. Before a large, late buffet dinner, six or seven canapés per guest is a good number to allow, and a variety is pleasant.

Here is a recipe for a dip borrowed from Mexico. It is pronounced Gwah-ka-mo-lay and should be served with chips or crackers.

GUACAMOLE

Mix 1 cup mashed avocado (2 med.), 1 tbsp. lemon juice, 1 tsp. salt, and 1½ tsp. grated onion. Either chopped tomato, crumbled Roquefort cheese, curry powder, chili powder, Worcestershire sauce, or Tabasco sauce may be added.

CHILI DIP

½ cup mayonnaise
½ cup sour cream
2 tbsp. chopped sweet
  pickles

1 tbsp. chopped stuffed
  olives
2 tsp. chili powder
1 tsp. paprika
1½ tsp. grated onion

Combine all ingredients. Cover and set aside in refrigerator 1 to 2 hours to chill and allow flavors to blend. Serve as dip with shrimp or cauliflowerets. *Makes about 1 cup.*

A dip popular with men has a pleasant tang of the sea, and the ingredients are always available even though you are 1,000 miles from an ocean. Here it is:

MINCED CLAM-CHEESE DIP

7½-oz. can minced clams, drained

two 3-oz. pkg. cream cheese

1 tbsp. lemon juice

1 tsp. Worcestershire sauce

½ tsp. salt

¼ tsp. flavor extender

⅛ tsp. ground pepper

Mix all ingredients.

Here is a recipe from old New Orleans.

SHRIMP REMOULADE

½ cup plus 2 tbsp. cooking (salad) oil

¼ cup Creole or prepared mustard

3 tbsp. vinegar

1 tsp. salt

¼ tsp. Tabasco sauce

2 tbsp. paprika

1 hard-cooked egg yolk

½ cup minced celery

2 tbsp. grated onion

2 tbsp. minced parsley

2 tbsp. minced green pepper

1 hard-cooked egg white, chopped

1 lb. shelled cooked shrimp

Beat oil, mustard, vinegar, salt, Tabasco sauce, paprika, and egg yolk with rotary beater until thick and blended. Fold in celery, onion, parsley, green pepper, and egg white. Mix with shrimp. Let stand in refrigerator several hours. Serve in cocktail glasses or on a platter garnished with lettuce leaves. *Makes about 1½ cups dressing.*

No doubt about it, the most impressive canapés are the hot ones, but resist them firmly unless you have help in the kitchen; or select those that may be prepared in advance and kept hot in a chafing dish without damage. Tiny Vienna sausages which may be speared with toothpicks and dipped into a sauce, or the bite-sized frozen canapé croquettes that need no more than thawing and heating, are good choices in this case.

One of my friends makes a hit with the tiny Swedish fishballs that come in glass. She browns them lightly in butter after rolling them in flour and keeps them sizzling in a chafing dish. Also for chafing-dish serving, she makes minute meat balls of equal parts of raw veal and cooked ham, ground, and quite highly seasoned.

One of my neighbors who has no help in the kitchen "hires" her twelve-year-old daughter and another sub-teenager to make and serve hot canapés by treating them to the movies once the party is well under way.

The little girls love this duty which lets them enjoy the start of a party, and brings them many well-deserved compliments.

One of their specialties is so exceptionally good and different that it has been on my star list since I first tasted it.

CHINESE WATER CHESTNUT CANAPÉS

Cut slices of bacon just long enough to encircle and overlap canned Chinese water chestnuts (or peeled uncooked fresh ones, if you can find them. Fresh ones are somewhat sweeter and crisper). Secure the bacon with a toothpick. Broil until crisp. Serve immediately with a small dish of East Indian chutney.

CHEESE KIX are easy to make. Melt ⅓ cup butter or margarine. Add 3 to 5 drops Tabasco sauce, ½ tsp. salt, 1 tsp. paprika, ⅓ cup grated dry American cheese, 4 cups Kix. Stir over low heat until well blended. Serve cold.

These same little girls turn out complicated tiny tart shells filled with creamed crab, or a rich, thick cheese rarebit that is especially toothsome in contrast to the hot flaky pastry. Their own favorite, possibly because they can ring in so many changes, is dainty, doll-sized pastry bites. Here is their recipe:

COCKTAIL SURPRISES

Make Short Pie dough (see directions on Bisquick pkg.) but mix in a bowl. Drain well button mushrooms or stuffed green olives; or use cocktail wieners, cocktail sausage, or an assortment of these. Wrap dough around foods just to cover. Dip tops in celery seeds or poppy seeds. Do this far ahead of time. When ready to serve, bake 8 to 10 minutes in hot oven (450°). *Makes 3 dozen.*

SAUTÉED ALMONDS

1 cup almonds	1 tsp. salt
2 tbsp. butter	½ tsp. ginger

Heat oven to 350° (moderate). Combine nuts and butter. Put in shallow pan and bake for 30 minutes until golden brown. Stir nuts occasionally. Drain on absorbent paper. Add salt and ginger. Toss with nuts.

1. Mushroom Canapés, **p. 47**
2. Ribbon Sandwiches
3. Chipped Beef and
   Cream Cheese Pinwheels
4. Cocktail Surprises, **p. 51**
5. Canapé Cream Puffs, **p. 47**
6. Wedges from Edam Cheese
7. Salami Cheese Cornucopias
8. Green Leaf Canapés, **p. 46**
9. Cheese Pastry Shells, **p. 136**
   On picks in Edam cheese:
10. Shrimp
11. Chinese Water Chestnut
    Canapés, **p. 50**
    (wrapped in bacon)
12. Minced Clam-Cheese Dip, **p. 49**
13. Chili Dip, **p. 48**

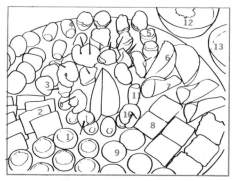

Key to picture on p. 140-141.

Tomato juice always is a happy choice with appetizers, but I like to vary it each time I serve it. Add celery or garlic salt, or Worcestershire sauce and lemon, or a slice of lime and a sprig of lightly crushed mint, or mix it half-and-half with clam juice, or undiluted chicken or beef bouillon.

MULLED CIDER

Boil together for 10 minutes 2 qt. sweet cider, 1 tsp. whole cloves, 1 tsp. whole allspice, a 3″ stick of cinnamon, ½ unpeeled lemon, thinly sliced, ¼ to ½ cup sugar. Strain and serve hot. Makes 16 half-cup servings.

If fruit juice is your choice before dinner, try the tart tang of cranberry juice on the rocks. Cold cider on the rocks is a refreshing summer drink. Hot Mulled Cider is a welcome start for a meal on a cold autumn day.

Even with the smallest group, a hostess has no time to spare at the start of a party, so appetizers that need last minute attention are a poor choice, unless there is help in the kitchen. Better skip hot canapés than abandon guests at the moment of arrival to hover over the oven!

Small Dinners

THERE IS A special warmth and charm about dinner served at a table. Certainly this is the most graceful way to entertain a few guests, particularly if they know each other well, or if you want them to become better acquainted with a newcomer to your group.

As a general thing, I find that six is about the most I can serve at table with ease if I am without help in the kitchen. For more than eight, I choose some kind of buffet service.

The choice of menu, advance preparation of food, and careful planning of service is important for any party. At no time is advance thought more vital to success than before the sit-down dinner. The hostess' absence is so much more conspicuous in a small group.

The attractiveness of the small dinner depends on its mood of serenity and easy, seemingly effortless, hospitality. Relaxation disappears with the hostess who is forever leaving the table to change plates, get more food, or check on the progress of something in the oven.

One of my friends uses two side tables, one by her husband and one by her place, as supplements to her small dining table. He serves the main course and takes care of the used plates on the lower shelf of his table. She serves salad and dessert from hers.

In order to avoid such interruptions of good talk, many hostesses I know skip a first course at the table and concentrate on appetizers in the living room, and main course and an elaborate dessert at the table.

One of the most useful pieces of furniture for the hostess who is serving her own sit-down dinner is a teacart. If the table is too small to accommodate a big platter in front of either host or hostess, main dishes may be served from the top of the teacart. Later, guests may be asked to pass their empty plates. These are stored, out of sight, on the lower shelf of the teacart; then the dessert and its plates are lifted to the table for serving. If hot bread is in a bread warmer, the hostess need never leave the table during dinner.

Women are directed to their seats first, though it is always best to do the easiest and simplest thing. Therefore, it is quite proper to say, "Jane, will you sit there? And George next to you. Then Phyllis . . ." especially when seating a big party, or if seating all women first leaves the men standing around uncertainly.

At dinner for four, the hostess need say no more than, "Alice, will you sit there?" indicating the chair to the host's right. This tells the male guest that he is expected to take the seat opposite her, on the right of the hostess.

When a single woman is entertaining another woman and two men, she places the woman opposite her.

At dinner for six, the hostess need direct only the woman she wants on the host's right to that place, and the man she wants at her right to his seat, though it is gracious to catch the eye of the other woman guest first and indicate her place at the host's left with a smile and a small wave of the hand.

At dinner for eight, another man is placed facing the host so that men and women are alternated around the table. The host never gives up his place at the head of his table. It is always the wife who takes a place on the side.

As the hostess seats herself, each man pulls out the chair for the woman on his right, gets her comfortably settled, and then seats himself.

The host does not leave the table to aid the hostess in removing plates to sideboard or kitchen since that would leave guests alone. The comparative stranger to the house should not offer to help, since that implies a criticism of the other, more intimate friends. A close woman friend may offer help, if it seems to be needed. I am always grateful to the guest who asks, "May I give you a hand?" rather than springing up to volunteer without a word. Her impulse is the kindest, but there are many times when it is far easier to deal with this task alone, especially if a kitchen is small and demands careful organization. And nothing but confusion results if all guests start milling to the kitchen with empty plates.

If the table is very small, it is better to forget butter plates and individual salad plates rather than crowd them into place. It is much wiser to concentrate on a graceful eye-catching centerpiece than to show off all items of a set of china, no matter how beautiful, if there is not enough space to display them to comfortable advantage.

Platters and other serving dishes should be in place near the server. Dinner plates should be in a pile in front of either host or hostess, depending on which is serving. Or dinner plates may be in place before guests and the serving dishes, if not unwieldly or very large, may be passed along from guest to guest, counter-clockwise around the table so that each may help himself in turn.

Some prefer to serve the hostess first so she may lead the way. Her plate is also removed first at the end of each course. Others serve the guest of honor first, continuing in order around the table.

At home, portions are smaller than in restaurants, since it is usual and hospitable to offer second helpings. Nothing is less attractive than an overloaded plate. One heaped high does not indicate a generous host so much as an inexperienced one! Have plenty for generous second helpings, though, and some to spare. Leftovers can always be saved, but a hungry guest is beyond help.

The hostess gives the sign to leave the table. She need do no more than lay her napkin beside her plate and start to rise at any time when no one is in the middle of conversation. Or she can say, "Shall we leave the table?" or "Are we ready for coffee? Let's have it in the living room."

Words that always embarrass me are "Shall we find more comfortable chairs?" If dining room chairs are rocky and uncomfortable, nothing is gained by calling attention to the fact. I feel that the best, most considerate rule is, "Give the best you have

The single woman may say, "Will you play host for me?" to any of her male guests, married or unmarried, when assigning him the place opposite her; but this should be an empty invitation. She does not ask him to carve or take on any other duties.

Final test for a party menu: make sure it does not demand the impossible of one oven. Disaster follows an attempt to broil a steak, roast potatoes, bake muffins, toast the top of a casserole, all at the same time.

without apology." The hostess who makes belittling comment about her china, or silver, or size of her house can only embarrass her guests—and turn the spotlight on some detail that may not have been noticed.

The most enjoyable small dinners are those that emphasize good food that is also easy to serve, even though it may have been hours in preparation.

An excellent example of a hearty, well-chosen menu for effortless serving was one I enjoyed recently. The main dish was a rolled roast of beef. The gravy had been made and the meat carved in the kitchen before guests arrived. The succulent slices were reassembled and kept warm until time to bring them to the table. They occupied the center of a large platter; around the edge were alternated bright carrots, whole white onions, and potatoes that had been cooked with the meat and were glazed a tempting brown. Small salads of tossed greens were at the left of each place, so all the host had to do was to serve each dinner plate and pass it along. Hot buttered rolls were passed from guest to guest in a basket.

At a small dinner, guests wait until the hostess lifts her fork for the first bite as a signal to begin. At a big dinner, the hostess frequently says, "Please start now," to guests served first, and when she makes this request they should do so.

The hostess left her place only once to remove dinner and salad plates to the kitchen and bring back a dramatic Apricot Mousse Supreme (p. 70) which she served from her place.

Dessert forks and spoons may be on the table, or the hostess may add the needed silver to each dessert plate as she serves it, whichever is the more convenient.

A party meal—or any other—should be a feast for the eye as well as the tongue. Therefore, the contrast of colors deserves the most careful thought. Mashed potatoes, creamed onions, turnips, and celery, peeled cucumbers, and breast of chicken are each delicious, but they look pallid and far from tempting assembled on the same plate.

A contrast in textures is another requirement for the meal that will bring compliments. A superbly smooth fish pudding or a lovely, cloudlike soufflé is doubly good when accompanied by a crisp salad rather than a molded one of bland texture, and by rolls with crunchy crusts rather than delicately soft ones.

Some very young hostesses make the mistake of trying to make every item in a party menu a knockout by seasoning and saucing each to the limit. Certainly each dish should be seasoned with imagination, but the most enjoyable meals are those that are designed as a whole, so that each item compliments, rather than rivals, the others. If a gravy is sharply seasoned with curry or

The hostess serving a meal without help does best not to follow the routine of a well-trained maid by offering each platter to the left of each guest. Service without a maid must be informal to some degree. That is part of its charm! It is better to be a relaxed hostess than to try to be both hostess and maid and do neither job well.

chili, it is often better to save that Spanish sauce that is so admired for the Lima beans, and that highly seasoned garlic bread for another occasion.

Here are some examples of well-planned menus for small dinners—nutritionally well-balanced, attractive in contrasts of colors, textures, and seasonings, and, what is of greatest importance, demanding very little last-minute attention. *Recipes for starred dishes will be found later in this book.*

Chilled Asparagus Tips with Mayonnaise
*Parmesan Oven-fried Chicken
*Olive Creamed Potatoes
Platter of Tomato Slices
with Chilled Ripe Olives
Warm Crescent Rolls
*Berry Basket Cake
Coffee

*Chilled Tomato and Cucumber Soup
*Stuffed Pork Chops
Julienne Green Beans with Smoky Salt
Baked Apple Rings
Parkerhouse Rolls
*Gay Nineties Charlotte Russe
Coffee

Relish Tray
Roast Prime Ribs of Beef
Parsley Buttered Potatoes
*Italian Broccoli
Hot Dinner Rolls
*French Silk Chocolate Puffs
Coffee

First Courses

If you are serving a first course, it is a great help to have it on the table before guests are seated. This means choosing one that can stand at room temperature for a short while, such as avocado (dipped in lemon juice), shrimp or crab cocktail, eggs à la russe, cold asparagus tips with mayonnaise, paper-thin slices of proscuitto or other very salty ham with mango or other melon in inch-wide slices.

One of the best first courses I know is this creamy, flavorsome mousse of a lovely pale green, served in individual molded portions.

AVOCADO MOUSSE

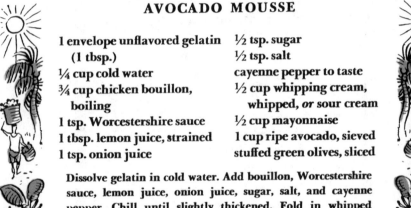

1 envelope unflavored gelatin (1 tbsp.)
¼ cup cold water
¾ cup chicken bouillon, boiling
1 tsp. Worcestershire sauce
1 tbsp. lemon juice, strained
1 tsp. onion juice
½ tsp. sugar
½ tsp. salt
cayenne pepper to taste
½ cup whipping cream, whipped, *or* sour cream
½ cup mayonnaise
1 cup ripe avocado, sieved
stuffed green olives, sliced

Dissolve gelatin in cold water. Add bouillon, Worcestershire sauce, lemon juice, onion juice, sugar, salt, and cayenne pepper. Chill until slightly thickened. Fold in whipped cream, mayonnaise, and avocado. Whip with rotary beater. Test for seasonings. Pour into 6 oiled ½-cup individual molds. Chill 3 hours. Unmold and serve on a lettuce leaf. Darker green leaves of the lettuce make a nice contrast. Garnish with a slice of green olive. *6 servings.*

In Western states, salad is often served as a first course. The hostess may serve a mixed green salad at the table, or have individual helpings of fancier salads in place.

A pimiento stuffed with grated green cabbage, highly seasoned mayonnaise, and chopped black olives is effective. So is a ring of green pepper heaped with a mixture of raw and cooked vegetables in thousand island dressing. A first-course salad I had recently is:

CELERY ROOT
AND GRAPE SALAD

*1 cup celery root
   (approx. 2 roots)
1 cup water
1 tsp. celery salt
¼ tsp. white pepper
1 tbsp. lemon juice
½ cup French dressing

2 cups seedless green grapes
   or halved seeded Tokay
   grapes
2 cups minted pineapple
   chunks
¼ cup slivered almonds, toasted
½ cup mayonnaise

Peel brown knobs of celery root. Dice in ½" squares. Simmer celery root in water seasoned with celery salt, white pepper, and lemon juice for 10 minutes. Drain; marinate in French dressing in the refrigerator 2 to 3 hours or overnight. When ready to serve, combine drained marinated celery root, chilled grapes and pineapple, slivered almonds, and mayonnaise. Toss lightly until all ingredients are coated with mayonnaise. Serve on lettuce leaves or watercress. Garnish with sprig of parsley or small bunch of Tokay grapes. *6 to 8 servings.*

*If celery root is not available, substitute 1 cup uncooked julienne celery for cooked celery root.

Cold soups are delightful, especially on a hot night, though I often serve them in the winter. They are a much more sensible choice than hot ones for the hostess running a party without help.

Jellied madrilene is always attractive, and adapts well to a very wide variety of main courses.

Cold cream of chicken, seasoned with curry and topped with chopped pimiento and green pepper, or toasted slivered almonds, is an appetizing and substantial start. Cold cream of spinach, water-

CELERY LOUISIANNE is a flavorsome first course. Quarter hearts of celery (no. 303 can). Cover with 10½-oz. can undiluted consommé; add ½ tsp. cracked pepper. Simmer uncovered, until liquid is reduced to a glaze. Marinate several hours in 1 cup French dressing seasoned with ½ tsp. anchovy paste. Serve on lettuce leaves.

cress, and asparagus soups take on a novel and rather peppery bite if finely minced raw celery tops and a little grated raw onion are added.

Vichyssoise is a great favorite. There are many recipes for this smooth potato soup, varying from elaborate ones calling for cream, cooked leeks, potatoes, onions, and curry powder to lighter and more quickly made ones such as the following:

VICHYSSOISE

| 1 can frozen condensed | ½ soup can milk |
| cream of potato soup | ½ soup can light cream |

In saucepan, heat soup, milk, and cream over low heat until soup is completely thawed. Beat until smooth with electric blender or rotary beater. Place in refrigerator for at least 4 hours. Serve in chilled bowls. *3 servings.* If you like extra seasoning, stir in dash of nutmeg, thyme, or Tabasco. For special garnish, use chopped chives, shredded vegetables, sliced olives, parsley, or shredded cheese.

Recently I had a cold soup that had the appearance of a creamed one. The first taste told me it wasn't, however. It had such a tempting tang I asked for the recipe. It turned out to be as simple to make as it was tasty. It is an especially good appetizer because of the slightly tart taste of the buttermilk.

CHILLED TOMATO AND CUCUMBER SOUP

1 tsp. Worcestershire sauce	2 cups buttermilk
½ tsp. curry powder	1 medium cucumber, chopped
10½-oz. can condensed cream of tomato soup	cracked black pepper

Combine Worcestershire sauce and curry powder. Stir into tomato soup. Add buttermilk slowly and stir until completely blended. Add cucumber. Chill thoroughly. Sprinkle cracked black pepper on top of each serving. *6 to 8 servings.*

With any soup, I like to offer something more novel than the usual crackers but different from the hot bread I like to serve with a main course. The following is one of my standbys:

CHEESE SNACKS

1 cup Bisquick	about ⅓ cup milk
½ cup grated sharp yellow cheese	½ cup chopped parsley or chives
2 tbsp. mayonnaise	1 tbsp. grated onion

Heat oven to 450° (hot). Blend thoroughly with fork Bisquick, cheese, mayonnaise, and milk. Shape into ½″ balls. Roll in mixture of parsley and onion. Bake on greased baking sheet *8 to 10 minutes. Makes about 30.*

One of the best cooks I know skips appetizers and serves her first course in the living room before small dinners.

"It really is a time-saver because I don't have to fuss with canapés or with changing first-course plates at the table," she says. "Also, it keeps my guests occupied with something to eat while I am in the kitchen dishing up my main course and getting it to the table. I join my guests with a small serving of the first course for myself, and slip out before they have finished to heat rolls and attend to other last minute duties."

Her first course is always something that can be assembled in advance on separate plates, such as an avocado half filled with mayonnaise and capers, or small aspics, or a crab ravigotte.

She hands a fork and dinner napkin with each plate. When her main course is on the table, she moves guests to the dining room by saying, "Shall we go in? Just leave plates, but will you bring your napkins?"

This is not the most formal service, certainly, but it is very practical and pleasant. Later, when she leaves the dining room briefly to get dessert or start coffee, she takes a minute or two to pile the first-course dishes on a tray and take them to the kitchen. This takes only an instant, but leaves the living room cleared as if by magic.

One of her most effective and easy first courses served in place of appetizers is artichokes, either chilled or at room temperature. Artichoke plates are a charming luxury, and most convenient because of the well for the sauce; but they are not at all necessary for serving this vegetable, once such a rarity but now so widely available. Artichokes may be served on any plate large enough to accommodate sauce, discarded leaves, and fork needed to remove the choke and eat the heart.

HEARTS OF PALM SALAD is delightful either with a meal or as a first course. This delicacy comes in cans from South America and the Philippines. Split the tender stalks, or cut them in rounds. Serve on lettuce garnished with orange slices and French dressing.

Heat oven to 400° (moderately hot). Wash chicken, drain and place skin-side-down in single layer in shallow baking pan. Mix rest of ingredients (except mushrooms) to make sauce and pour over each piece of chicken, coating well. Bake *45 minutes*, basting occasionally. Turn, sprinkle mushrooms over top, baste again with sauce, and bake *15 minutes longer*. Remove chicken to hot platter and spoon sauce over top. *4 to 6 servings.* (For crisp chicken, bake at 425°.)

Chinese Veal takes little time to prepare.

CHINESE VEAL

1 lb. cubed veal
2 tbsp. hot fat
2 onions, cut finely (1 cup)
½ cup uncooked rice
11-oz. can condensed chicken-rice soup *or* 2 chicken bouillon cubes dissolved in 1 cup boiling water

¼ cup soy sauce
1 cup water
1 cup celery, cut finely
1 pkg. frozen peas (or no. 2 can)
about ¼ cup toasted almonds

Heat oven to 425° (hot). Brown veal in hot fat. Add onions and sauté until golden. Pour the browned veal and onion, rice, soup, soy sauce, and water into 2-qt. baking dish. Cover and bake *40 minutes*. Uncover and add celery and peas. Cover and bake *20 minutes more*. Sprinkle with almonds. *6 servings.*

A hearty, attractive main dish, particularly good in the crisp autumn is:

STUFFED PORK CHOPS WITH PINEAPPLE-ORANGE DRESSING

6 double pork chops
2 cups dry bread crumbs (about 3 slices)
1 tsp. salt
dash of pepper
½ tsp. dried marjoram
¼ cup chopped celery (leaves and stalks)

2 tbsp. finely minced onion
2 tbsp. butter or margarine, melted
9-oz. can crushed pineapple, well drained (about ½ cup)
2 tsp. grated orange rind

Have pork chops cut with pocket on bone side. Trim off excess fat. Toss crumbs and seasonings together. Add remaining ingredients; toss lightly to blend. Spoon dressing lightly into pockets of pork chops. Brown chops slowly on both sides. Season with salt and pepper. Add few drops of water, just enough to prevent scorching. Cover. Cook slowly on top of range or bake in moderate oven (350°) for 1 hour 15 minutes to 1½ hours. *6 servings.*

Vegetables

I try to give vegetables special attention for party serving.

Lima beans, tossed with butter and lemon juice just before serving, are a useful, easily prepared party dish. Green beans take on character if cooked in bouillon, or in a small amount of water heavily seasoned with smoked salt.

Few people rush for a second helping of boiled carrots, but I find them very popular if grated, sautéed briefly with butter and salt in a skillet until they are steaming hot but still slightly crisp, and served with a dusting of nutmeg.

As a general rule, vegetables that have a strong aroma during cooking are best avoided in a party menu unless they can be prepared well in advance. Broccoli, steamed in the morning until almost done, releases most of its strong odor. Unless overcooked, it suffers not at all from reheating at the last minute.

ITALIAN BROCCOLI

Cook 1 pkg. frozen broccoli until almost tender. Drain. Sauté in 3 tbsp. hot olive oil until delicately browned. Sprinkle with 2 tbsp. Parmesan cheese. *4 to 5 servings.*

A whole head of firm white cauliflower makes a pretty appearance at the table. It will not announce its presence to your guests as they enter the door, if steamed in an inch of water until almost tender several hours before needed. Just before serving, reheat. Drain. Center it on a serving platter. Cover with a thick cream sauce sharply seasoned with grated yellow cheese. I sometimes serve this ringed with green peas or green beans.

Other vegetable recipes, particularly pleasant for party serving, will be found under Buffet Dinners.

Desserts

People think first of a wonderful dessert when they say "party." Certainly desserts are a most important part of any meal, and are doubly successful if dramatically served.

One of my friends whose favorite dessert is fresh fruit and cheese makes a centerpiece of the fruit, heaped around four tall candlesticks on a long narrow rectangle of mirror cut for that purpose. The table looks beautiful when we sit down, with yellow pears, polished red apples, plums, peaches, cherries, green grapes, or any other fruits in season arranged on green leaves.

A trifle, delicate cake, chiffon pie, or a molded dessert are good choices after a substantial meal. The following recipe makes a rich dessert, but it seems light and is so good that I asked for the recipe.

APRICOT MOUSSE SUPREME

2 tbsp. unflavored gelatin (2 envelopes)
¼ cup cold water
2 cups whipping cream
1 cup *sifted* confectioners' sugar

2 tsp. grated lemon rind
¼ tsp. salt
1½ cups sieved stewed apricots
2 tbsp. lemon juice

Soften gelatin in cold water. *Dissolve over hot water until thin and clear. Add confectioners' sugar, lemon rind, and salt to whipping cream. Begin whipping the cream. Just as cream begins to thicken, add dissolved gelatin in a thin stream. Continue beating until stiff. Fold in apricots and lemon juice. Pour into well greased 1½-qt. mold. Chill in freezer 2 to 3 hours until firm. When ready to serve, run spatula around edge of mold. Dip in bowl of hot water a few seconds and invert on serving plate. Garnish with halves of fresh or canned apricots and lemon or galax leaves. Serve immediately. *6 to 8 servings.*

*To dissolve gelatin use small custard cup or measuring cup and set in pan of boiling water.

One of the most impressive, spectacular desserts is Baked Alaska. We think of this as being so elaborate and demanding of close last-minute attention that it should not be attempted by any but professional chefs. Good news! Here is a way to make it in advance by a method so simple that even the inexpert cook can safely choose it for the triumph of a small dinner. Perhaps you will want to serve this later in the living room with coffee.

BAKED ALASKA ANGEL FOOD CAKE

Bake cake in tube pan as directed on package of Betty Crocker Angel Food Cake Mix. When thoroughly cool, remove from pan, cut out 1″ of cake from center, and fill center with 1 qt. *softened* ice cream. Wrap immediately with freezer-weight paper such as aluminum foil, cellophane, or Pliofilm. Freeze. When ready to use, unwrap and put on board (wrap board with aluminum foil to protect it from heat). Cover ice cream filled cake with Betty Crocker Meringue Mix made by beating 2 packets of mix with ⅔ cup water until stiff. Place in 500° oven (very hot) for about 5 minutes until meringue is delicately browned. Allow to stand ½ hour out of oven before serving, and the ice cream will be just ready to eat.

Another rich and unusual dessert is:

COLONIAL INNKEEPER'S PIE

Pastry

1 cup *sifted* GOLD MEDAL Flour
½ tsp. salt

⅓ cup lard (or ⅓ cup plus 1 tbsp. hydrogenated shortening)
2 tbsp. water

Mix flour and salt. Cut in shortening. Sprinkle with water. Mix with fork until all flour is moistened. Round into ball. Roll pastry 1" larger than inverted 9" pie pan. Ease into pan; flute high on pie crust edge. Cover with pliofilm and put aside while preparing sauce and batter.

Sauce

1½ sq. unsweetened chocolate (1½ oz.)
½ cup water

⅔ cup sugar
¼ cup butter
1½ tsp. vanilla

Melt chocolate with water; add sugar. Bring to boil, stirring constantly. Remove from heat; stir in butter and vanilla. Set aside.

Batter

1 cup *sifted* GOLD MEDAL Flour
¾ cup sugar
1 tsp. baking powder
½ tsp. salt

¼ cup shortening
½ cup milk
½ tsp. vanilla
1 egg
½ cup finely chopped nuts

Heat oven to 350° (moderate). Sift dry ingredients together. Add shortening, milk, and vanilla. Beat 2 minutes, medium speed on mixer or 300 vigorous strokes by hand. Scrape sides and bottom of bowl constantly. Add egg. Beat 2 more minutes, scraping bowl constantly. Pour batter into prepared pie pan. Stir sauce and pour carefully over cake batter. Sprinkle top with nuts. Bake *55 to 60 minutes,* or until toothpick stuck in center comes out clean. Garnish with whipped cream or whipped ice cream. *8 servings.*

After Dinner Coffee

COFFEE IS NOT served with the main course of any dinner that makes the slightest claim to formality. However, it is absurd not to do so if you enjoy coffee with a meal instead of later.

"Joe likes coffee with dinner. Will you join him, or have it later with me?" asked one of my friends recently as she started to the kitchen to serve her main course.

As it happened, none of her guests cared for coffee until after dinner, so she served her husband and the table was not cluttered with the large cups that were not needed.

It was thoughtful of her to make sure of our wishes, and she saved confusion by inquiring in advance. If coffee is served to one person with the main course, it should be offered to all. On the other hand, if it is not offered, the considerate guest does not ask for it, no matter how welcome it would be.

My heart went out in sympathy to a hostess who was asked, after we were seated at the table, "Do you mind if I have coffee now?" by what I can only label as a thoughtless or a most inexperienced guest.

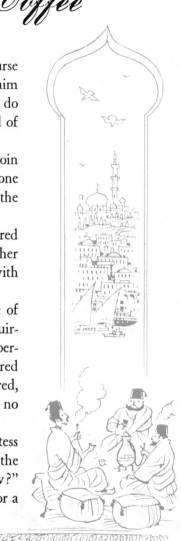

EGG COFFEE. Beat 1 egg and 2 tbsp. water. Stir 2 tbsp. of the egg mixture into ¾ cup regular grind coffee. Add cold water to completely moisten grounds. Put in coffeepot and add 6 cups cold fresh water. Stir. Bring to full boil. Stir again. Remove from heat. Add dash of cold water. Strain and serve. Makes 6 to 8 cups coffee.

I happened to know that our hostess had taken particular pains to organize her service in advance. She had planned to turn on heat under her coffee-maker when she went out to get dessert so that it would be ready for serving in demitasses in the living room after we had finished her carefully planned dinner.

"Well, of course," she said smoothly, though she could not have been happy at leaving the table, starting coffee, leaving again when it was ready, returning with large cup, teaspoon, cream, and sugar —and neglecting five people for the pleasure of one.

ARCTIC COOLER. Here is a variation of iced coffee for a hot night. Make double-strength coffee and chill. To 4 cups add ½ cup sifted confectioners' sugar and 2½ tsp. vanilla. Stir. Add ⅛ tsp. cinnamon and dash of nutmeg to ½ cup whipping cream. Just before serving, whip until stiff. Pour coffee into chilled glasses filled with coffee ice cubes. Top with whipped cream. 6 servings.

If coffee is served in regular coffee cups, it is poured at the table (or at a sideboard) when dessert is served. Cream and sugar are put on the table at the hostess' right and passed along to the guests. Coffee in regular-size cups usually is not served after you leave the table.

Coffee in demitasses may be served at the table, following dessert, or after you leave the table.

Coffee in the living room is a graceful and most convenient ceremony. For one thing, the pretty little cups need not match each other, though, of course, a matching service is more formal.

One of my friends has been collecting exquisite Victorian demitasses for years. A tray of them of many colors, shapes, and designs is a charming sight and a good conversation piece. Her collection started with one charmer inherited from her grandmother. The rest were gifts. Each has a history and a special association. They afford an easy way to turn conversation in many directions. "I'll give you the cup that came from Boston because you've just been there," she said to me recently leading talk to a current trip.

The little cups with their tiny spoons, sugar, and cream are assembled on a tray in advance. Coffee may be served in a classic silver pot, or in any container that looks festive.

Trays carrying coffee and tea services are used bare rather than covered with a cloth.

The hostess may set the tray before her on a coffee table, and add cream and sugar, if needed, to each cup as she fills it. In this case, the host or some helpful male guest aids her by handing cups to guests beyond her reach.

Women are served first, starting with the guest of honor or any woman very much older than the others.

If the group is large, all cups may be filled and the whole tray with cream and sugar passed by either host or hostess. In this case, women are not served first. The tray is offered to each guest in turn around the circle.

Lump sugar usually is not served with demitasses since many people prefer only the smallest amount of sugar in the small portions.

"I am not going to serve cream. It isn't *supposed* to be added to after-dinner coffee," I heard a very young bride declare recently.

I liked her mother's mild answer.

"What are you trying to do? Please your guests—or train them?" she said with a smile.

It is true that the connoisseur of coffee does not add cream to the traditional "small black" served in demitasses, but I never fail to have cream ready for those who enjoy it, and quite a few

SESAME HONEY DEMITASSE is good for those who like sweetened coffee. Boil 1 cup water, 2 tbsp. sesame seeds, 2 tbsp. honey. Cover and simmer 5 minutes. Remove from heat and add 1½ tbsp. powdered instant coffee. Strain into demitasse cups. 4 servings.

CAFÉ MEXICAIN. Mix into ½ cup whipping cream ⅛ tsp. ground cinnamon, ⅛ tsp. nutmeg, and 1 tbsp. confectioners' sugar. Just before serving whip until stiff. Top six cups strong, hot black coffee with this mixture.

of my friends do. The thoughtful hostess also keeps a jar of instant caffeine-free coffee on hand for any guests who love the taste of coffee after a meal but fear to drink it in the evening.

There are as many ways to make coffee as there are hostesses. I think it is fun to experiment. Here are some of the secrets I picked up from hostesses all over the country:

Try a tiny dash of salt and a very light powdering of cinnamon in the pot before pouring in hot coffee. The proper amount is best determined by experiment. The cinnamon flavor should be barely discernible.

Try adding a teaspoonful of unsweetened chocolate and a dash of salt to six cups of strong coffee. The chocolate flavor is not apparent, but it adds a subtle richness to the coffee flavor. The tiniest sprinkling of monosodium glutamate will also step up the flavor.

Try twisting a bit of orange peel, just enough to release the zest, over each cup. The peel is not served.

Above all, try different brands and processes. A New Orleans friend regularly sends me chicory coffee which I sometimes mix with a lighter blend, though I find it also delightful "so strong it stains the cup," as they like it in the Deep South.

It is not customary to serve anything with after dinner coffee in demitasses, but bonbons or mints may be passed and are a pleasant accompaniment.

Buffet Dinners

"BUFFET" IS THE name of a piece of furniture. Common usage has turned the word into an adjective meaning "serve yourself."

If I had to choose one form of entertaining only, I would choose buffet service. It is the most adaptable of events. You can serve four or forty gracefully with much less help, space, and equipment than needed for an equal number of guests at the table, so long as you proceed with caution in choice of foods.

The variety of dishes suitable for buffet service is enormous. Actually, almost any of the party foods I am discussing in other chapters in this book may be served buffet style. However, the best ones for the hostess without help, have several things in common.

They may be carved and otherwise prepared for service in advance.

They do not suffer from being kept hot over a chafing dish flame, or from standing, unheated, until time for second helpings.

They may be cooked in advance. One of my friends puts this tellingly. "I look at a recipe, and if it can't be made the day before,

I turn the page. It may be wonderful—but it's no use to me for a buffet."

The best start for a party of any kind is: First, careful choice of menu; second, a complete shopping list; and third, a careful plan of the whole day so that each duty is finished in easy time.

At the risk of being tiresome, I repeat my council, "Make lists!" Unless you do so, you may find yourself in a flurry, setting the table with silver that is dingy and must be shined in those precious last moments you had set aside for yourself to shower and dress.

One of my friends has a house that always looks immaculate, furniture and silver gleaming. She smiled when I asked her about her routine of housework before her parties.

"I'll tell you a secret," she said. "I get ready for two big parties in two big days. I have a cleaning woman who comes to me once a week. On Thursday, she does windows, floors, furniture, napkins, and tablecloths while I shine every piece of silver in the house, order what I need for my parties, bake cakes and the fancy breads I have scheduled, and attend to any other food preparation I have time for. On Friday, I concentrate on the buffet dinner for that night, but cooking enough of certain dishes so that I will have leftovers I need for a completely different dinner for six or eight on Saturday. The big pieces of silver stay gleaming. Once over lightly with the vacuum cleaner restores the house to order. My husband helps me with the dishes. And after my buffet I am practically ready for the next party, so far as food is concerned."

This is a rather heroic schedule for most hostesses, but her plan to prepare her house two days before a party and keep the day itself free for cooking and setting her table is a sound one.

In setting the table for buffet service, it is important to arrange dishes so that guests can proceed past the table without back tracking. Plates, knives, forks, and napkins should be at one extreme end rather than in the middle. Place any dish that needs a sauce in advance of its garnishing so that rice, for example, is on the plate before the guest arrives at the gravy meant to top it.

Water usually is not served with a buffet meal. If cider, iced tea, or any other drink is served, glasses may be waiting, filled, at the farthest end of the table to be picked up last. Very frequently, the host circulates with a tray of beverages after everyone is seated.

Guests usually are allowed to find their own places in the living room after helping themselves, though the thoughtful hostess is alert to direct a stranger to a congenial group by saying something such as, "Sylvia, sit here by Pete. He's just back from Colorado and can answer your questions about skiing at Aspen."

In a small apartment, four or six will naturally draw up around a coffee table and use it for cups and glasses. The hostess who has more space and who entertains in buffet fashion often will find small collapsible tables invaluable. While guests are serving themselves, these can be whipped into place in a matter of moments.

In a really spacious house, or one that has big comfortable porches, card tables may be scattered through the rooms. In this case, they are covered with cloths and set with silver, napkins, salt, and pepper. Guests choose their own places, but host and hostess always sit at different tables. Otherwise, the couple with them would seem to be honored exclusively above other guests.

Eight or twelve can pleasantly help themselves from a sideboard and then take seats at a dining table set with silver and cold beverage already in place. In this case the hostess usually lets guests

find places without direction, though the aware guest does not choose either the head or the foot of the table, and takes care to help by alternating men and women.

Announcing that a buffet dinner is ready is done casually. The woman guest of honor need not be invited to start first, especially if she is at that moment deep in an animated conversation. The hostess catches the eyes of several guests and says, "Marie, will you start for me? Tom, Joe, Ann—are you ready for dinner?" Other guests are expected to follow without additional invitation, a few at a time, so there is not a traffic jam but also no great delay past the table.

While guests are serving themselves, the hostess has a few minutes to empty ash trays, gather up canapé napkins, plates, and glasses, put salt and pepper shakers in convenient reach, open small tables if she is using them so that everything is cleared and ready for guests as they come back with filled plates.

She serves herself last. If she is experienced, she takes what is only the first of a series of very small helpings. If she is taking care of a big party, she has time for only about half of her own dinner before slipping out to bring in reserves for second helpings. Then she can finish her own meal with a free mind before removing the main course plates.

This usually is not much of a problem. One or more guests intimate in the house usually volunteer to help, though the good guest knows that if everyone helps there is apt to be chaos in the kitchen. One or two assistants is enough!

Very often the hostess serves the dessert herself with help from host or a guest. She brings a cake, pie, ice cream, or whatever is her final course in a serving plate to the table or a convenient sideboard, cuts it, puts helpings on a dessert plate with fork or spoon, and sends in two at a time with her husband or one of those valued volunteer helpers who always seem to turn up when needed.

 *Main Dishes*

The experienced hostess thinks twice about choosing any dish that needs last-minute carving even if it may be cooked and garnished hours before guests are due.

A whole ham, gleaming under pineapple rings, is a royal sight in the middle of a candle-lit table. A turkey, succulently browned right out of the oven, is an impressive sight as you bear it in to your daintily set buffet. But what follows such moments of triumph nearly always is trouble.

It takes at least ten minutes for even the most expert carver to deal with a big bird. This means that the host will be busy with that duty while the hostess also is away from their guests as she attends to the few small things that always must be done at the last minute no matter how well in advance foods have been prepared.

If you must carve, plan something that can be carved in the kitchen before guests arrive, and reassembled or otherwise arranged attractively for serving so that it looks as tempting as it tastes.

Above all, don't draft a male guest at the last minute to carve for you at a buffet table, or the appearance of your table may be wrecked, and your roast as well.

Every man is not an expert carver, and some of the experts need more elbow room than a well-arranged buffet affords. However,

Ham is best cooked in the morning or even the day before a party. It may be carved in advance and slices returned to place if it is then wrapped in foil. This prevents slices drying and curling.

for some curious reason, it seems embarrassing to some men to admit any diffidence or inexperience about carving. Too many will say, "Certainly, if you want to take a chance on me," if asked. The result of such well-meant effort may well be a hot, unhappy guest and a table littered with crumbs of dressing, shreds of meat that have spilled off the platter, and an unsightly framework of what was so beautiful an uncarved bird or roast in the middle of your buffet.

This does not mean that you cannot plan a buffet dinner around such classic standbys as ham and turkey. This combination is among the most popular of main dishes for a large group for several good reasons. Everyone likes one or both. You can order bigger ones than you need with a free mind because some of the most delightful dishes may be made from the leftovers, and you can confidently expand your guest list at the last minute with the hospitable words, "By all means bring your house guest—there's plenty."

Because ham and turkey are popular main dishes for buffets, the clever hostess makes an effort to give them individual character.

Here is a turkey stuffing that is so very good you will be wise to make far more than can be contained in the bird. You'll need it!

Turkey is toothsome served hot, at room temperature, or cold. Under any circumstances, slices retain their juices and carve most easily if the bird is allowed to stand for at least 15 minutes after roasting.

STUFFING ELEGANTÉ

1 lb. chestnuts (about 2 cups), chopped
10½-oz. can beef bouillon
½ lb. bulk pork sausage
¼ cup sausage drippings
1 cup butter, melted
10 cups finely crumbled fresh bread

¾ cup onion, finely minced
1½ cups celery, chopped (stalks and leaves)
1 tbsp. marjoram
2 tsp. salt
½ to ¾ tsp. pepper
1 cup white raisins

With a sharp knife slit the skin on flat side of chestnuts. Place chestnuts in saucepan and cover with water. Bring to a boil. Remove chestnuts, one at a time from water. With sharp pointed knife remove shells and inner skins. Cook shelled chestnuts in beef bouillon for 25 minutes, or until tender. Drain. Chop nuts coarsely. Brown sausage in skillet, reserving ¼ cup of the drippings. Combine sausage drippings and butter. Add onions to butter-dripping mixture and sauté until onions are yellow, stirring occasionally. Mix in some of the bread crumbs, stirring to prevent excessive browning. Turn into a deep bowl and lightly mix in celery, marjoram, salt, pepper, and remaining crumbs. Add browned sausage, chestnuts, and raisins. Toss all ingredients together thoroughly. Cool and stuff turkey. If extra stuffing is left over bake in shallow pan or wrap in foil. Place in oven last 30 to 45 minutes of baking time. *Makes 3 qt. of dressing*, enough for a 12-lb. turkey.

During the hour before guests arrive, partially carve the bird in the kitchen. Slice the breast carefully, and put the thin even slices back in place so that your bird appears whole. Do the same with the legs without disjointing them. The host or guests will finish the carving, if necessary, when second helpings are due. Additional carving may not be needed. Time and again I have observed a curious fact about buffet meals. Though guests return for second and third helpings, food goes much farther when served from a buffet than at a table.

Cover the carved bird with foil and return it to the warm oven until time to heat rolls and the additional dressing. Serve gravy and additional dressing piping hot, and don't worry about reheating the turkey. It will look and taste delicious just as it is.

Ham is delicious served at room temperature, though many people prefer it chilled. Most important is to choose some kind of a topping that does not fall apart in carving, and to avoid those inches of cold, white fat that always are left on the plate. Here is a topping that I found especially tempting on a precooked ham that needed a relatively short baking time.

what's sauce for the goose is sauce for the gander

WASHINGTON CHERRY HAM GLAZE
(Pictured on p. 39.)

Heat oven to 350° (moderate). Score the ham diagonally into 1" squares. Make glaze by combining juice from 1 can cherry pie filling (reserving cherries for garnish), 1 cup orange marmalade with rind, and ½ cup sherry flavoring. Pour over ham and bake allowing 12 to 14 minutes per pound. Baste often.

There are exceptions to every rule. Recently I saw a large leg of lamb carved with greatest ease at a buffet table by an entirely in-experienced carver. The meat had been boned before roasting. It was stuffed with a forcemeat, or meat stuffing, so good it brought demands for the recipe from every guest. Here it is:

STUFFED LEG OF LAMB

Ask the butcher to bone a leg of lamb, leaving about 3" of shank bone in place so that the roast will retain its characteristic shape.

½ lb. ground raw veal
½ lb. ground cooked lean ham
½ cup fine dry bread crumbs
½ lb. raw mushrooms, finely chopped
1 egg

1 tsp. salt
¼ tsp. pepper
½ tsp. oregano
1 small clove garlic, crushed
1 tbsp. Worcestershire sauce
1 tbsp. orange marmalade, with rind

Heat oven to 325° (slow moderate). Mix all ingredients with hands until smooth and compact. Pack tightly into lamb leg. Sew up opening with heavy kitchen string or if stuffing is exposed, cover with aluminum foil and wrap with string to hold in place. Place fat-side-up in an open pan on a rack. Bake *about 20 minutes per lb.* if you prefer lamb on the pink side, or *30 to 35 minutes per lb.* if you prefer lamb well done.

Main dishes for buffet dinners need not be expensive to win compliments if some imagination is used to make simple ingredients seem partylike. A bride I know who runs her house on a very limited budget, and whose time is limited because she holds a job, has great success with a baked bean casserole. She assembles this the evening before a party. Brown and rye bread, and a large salad of grated cabbage complete her main course.

BAKED BEAN AND SAUSAGE CASSEROLE
(Pictured on p. 40.)

1 pkg. frozen Lima beans	1 tbsp. salt
three no. 303 cans baked beans	½ tsp. pepper
	½ tsp. dry mustard
two no. 2 cans kidney beans, drained	8-oz. can tomato sauce
	½ cup catsup
1 lb. Italian link sausage or pork link sausage	¼ cup brown sugar (packed)
½ lb. smoked ham	1 medium onion, chopped

Follow directions on Lima bean package except, cook only 10 minutes. Drain and gently mix with baked beans and kidney beans. Place sausage in skillet; add small amount of water. Cover and simmer 5 minutes. Drain. Pan fry until brown. Don't prick. Cut each sausage link into 2 or 3 pieces. *Heat oven to 400°* (moderately hot). Cut ham into ½" cubes. Add sausage and ham to beans. Combine seasonings, tomato sauce, catsup, brown sugar, and onion; add to beans. Pour bean mixture into 3-qt. baking dish. Bake *uncovered 1 hour. 10 to 12 servings.*

Another of this same girl's specialties is her own version of an always popular Italian dish. It can be assembled at any time and frozen until needed. All it needs is 30 minutes in a 350° (moderate oven) *after thawing*. With it she serves a big green salad with frozen artichoke hearts and bits of anchovy in French dressing, garlic bread, and a dessert, such as an elaborate fruit mold, that can be made the night before. Here is the recipe:

LASAGNE

(Pictured on p. 144.)

Make Tomato Sauce (recipe below). Meanwhile, cook ½ lb. lasagne noodles according to directions on package. Drain. Prepare Meat Balls (recipe below). Brown in hot fat, add a small amount of water, cover, and simmer 30 minutes. Place the following ingredients in layers in 13 x 9″ oblong pan in order listed, beginning and ending with the sauce. Repeat until all ingredients are used.

sauce
single layer of noodles
mixture of:
    ¾ lb. Ricotta cheese
      or cottage cheese
    1 tbsp. parsley

1 tsp. oregano
¾ cup grated Parmesan
    cheese
¾ lb. Mozzarella cheese,
    grated

Bake *30 minutes* in *moderate oven* (350°). Let stand 15 minutes, cut in squares and serve with Meat Balls. *6 to 8 servings.*

TOMATO SAUCE

Sauté ½ cup chopped onion, 1 clove garlic, minced, in 3 tbsp. olive oil. Add 2 no. 2 cans tomatoes, rubbed through sieve, 8-oz. can tomato sauce, 6-oz. can tomato paste, 1 cup water, 1 tsp. basil, 2 tbsp. minced parsley, 2 tsp. salt, ¼ tsp. pepper. Simmer over low heat 1 hour.

MEAT BALLS

Mix lightly and shape into 1″ balls:

¾ lb. ground beef
¼ lb. ground pork
1 cup fine dry bread
    crumbs
½ cup grated Parmesan
    cheese

1 tbsp. minced parsley
1 clove garlic, cut fine
½ cup milk
2 eggs, beaten
1½ tsp. salt
⅛ tsp. pepper

Among happiest choices for a main hot dish are well-seasoned ragouts and other dishes in which meat is cooked in bite-sized or smaller pieces. One that is very popular with both men and women, and rewarding to the busy hostess since it can be made a day in advance and improved by waiting, is Beef Stroganoff.

Curries are another main course that may be made well in advance, and they are one of the best ways I know to give leftover roast veal, pork, lamb, chicken, or turkey the look of a real party spread. The small bowls of crisp crumbled bacon, chopped peanuts, grated coconut, chopped onion, shredded pineapple, minced sweet pickles, and gingery chutney fill up the table—and the guests as well! Plenty of fluffy white rice and a lightly seasoned salad of delicate green such as Bibb lettuce or Belgian endive are the only accompaniments needed, and fruit is the classic dessert with curries. A good choice is melon balls, sliced peaches, canned pears, and frozen raspberries crushed with sugar or honey.

Creamed dishes are easy-to-serve main courses, since the sauce can be made in advance, combined with cooked sweetbreads, shrimp, lobster, crab, or chicken, and served in patty shells or over rice. Creamed dishes usually star at lunch or late supper rather than at a buffet dinner unless it is designed for women, as men generally like heartier fare at dinner.

Smorgasbord

The main course need not be hot to be hearty, however. One of the best ways I know to please a large crowd is a Smorgasbord. In Scandinavian countries the Smorgasbord is a prelude to a meal, but here in America we often see it served as a complete dinner. Everything can be put on the table before guests arrive. The variety of foods can be so large that it is sure to please every taste, and very nearly everything left over can be turned to good account later for sandwiches and snacks.

Instruct your guests to choose a first course from centerpiece dishes which contain delicacies in the appetizer class. These might be any choice you care to make of pickled herring in cream, shrimp marinated in garlic French dressing, anchovies, smoked salmon, stuffed eggs, cottage cheese, celery filled with cheese, large black olives, pickled beets, mustard onions, button mushrooms, small whole sweet pickles, lobster salad, and fish in aspic.

Delicious bread is essential to the success of a Smorgasbord. The very name means literally sandwich table. So make a feature of your bread baskets. Heap one with thinnest slices of a rich firm-grained loaf. In others, arrange limpa, rye, knackerbrod, homemade white, or any other substantial breads. Whipped or unsalted butter is a good choice with this meal.

For their main course guests return for helpings of less salty dishes, such as a combination of any of the following: Sliced smoked tongue, meat loaf, poached salmon in mayonnaise, jellied chicken, head cheese, potato, macaroni, or cooked vegetable salad. There should also be a choice of light salads, such as sliced cucumbers, tossed greens, sliced tomatoes, and tomato aspic and, of course, a large crystal bowl of Swedish Fruit Soup. If you want one or two hot dishes, Swedish meat balls in gravy and brown beans are good.

A suitable third course, which also should be in place at the start of the meal, is a molded fruit gelatin and an assortment of cheeses—Swiss, caraway, Gouda, Gjetost, or any others you fancy. Root beer and coffee are also served.

Vegetables

When I am serving a buffet meal, I choose vegetables that can be served from the casseroles in which they were cooked, or that are prepared individually because they look so handsome.

Small baked stuffed tomatoes are an example.

Bell peppers, baked with a Spanish rice filling, are an effective way to serve two foods combined.

Squash Continental is full of savor.

SQUASH CONTINENTAL

Cut 8 small zucchini squash into ½″ rounds. Sauté in ¼ cup butter, melted, 2 tsp. water, 1 clove garlic, crushed, ½ tsp. salt, and ⅛ tsp. pepper. Cook, covered, in saucepan with tight-fitting lid 6 to 8 minutes. Serve squash while still crisp. *6 to 8 servings*. Do not overcook as squash becomes soggy and loses its shape.

Tomatoes are colorful and tasty served in this manner:

BAKED STUFFED TOMATOES

6 tomatoes
½ cup chopped broiled
    bacon
¼ cup chopped celery
1 small onion, minced

1 cup soft bread crumbs
½ tsp. salt
½ cup grated cheese
6 tsp. butter

Heat oven to 350° (moderate). Wash tomatoes, but do not peel. Cut slice from top of each, scoop out centers and lightly salt insides. Mix tomato pulp, bacon, celery, onion, bread crumbs, salt, and ½ of cheese. Fill tomato cavities with mixture. Cover with remaining cheese. Dot with butter. Place in greased muffin cups or greased baking dish. Bake *about 30 minutes. 6 servings.*

GREEN BEANS IN SOUR CREAM always demand second helpings. Just before serving, mix hot drained beans thoroughly with sour cream, grated raw onions, and a squeeze of lemon.

Sweet potatoes are a good choice with ham. Here is a recipe I use often when I want a touch of sweet in a main course.

MARSHMALLOW-DATE SWEET POTATOES

4 medium sweet potatoes
9-oz. can (no. 1 flat)
   crushed pineapple
¼ cup butter
1 egg, slightly beaten
2 tsp. salt
1 tsp. nutmeg

18 dates, cut up
2 tbsp. brown sugar
2 tbsp. butter
8 marshmallows, quartered
   or 32 miniature
   marshmallows

Wash and cut out woody portion of sweet potatoes. Do not pare. Cook covered in 1" boiling salted water, 30 to 40 minutes until tender. Pare and mash.

Heat oven to 350° (moderate). Combine potatoes, pineapple, ¼ cup butter, egg, salt, nutmeg, and dates. Beat with spoon or electric mixer until creamy; spoon into an 8" round baking dish. Sprinkle with brown sugar and dot with 2 tbsp. butter. Top with marshmallows. Bake *uncovered 30 minutes,* until marshmallows are golden brown. *6 to 8 servings.*

In planning buffet meals, don't forget baked fruits as pleasant surprises with a main course.

Big canned peach halves brushed with softened or melted butter and broiled just long enough to heat and brown, are especially good with chicken. If desired, fill centers with red or green jelly.

OLIVE CREAMED POTATOES

6 medium-sized potatoes, boiled

2 cups commercial sour cream

3 tbsp. finely chopped onion

2 tbsp. finely chopped pimiento stuffed olives

1 tsp. salt

½ tsp. pepper

½ tsp. paprika

1 tbsp. chopped parsley

Dice potatoes. Pour cream into skillet; add potatoes. Heat slowly over medium heat until cream bubbles over potatoes. Add onion and olives. When potatoes are thoroughly heated, add salt and pepper. Serve at once, garnished with paprika and parsley. *6 servings.*

Salads

Tossed green salads are hard to beat for popularity and taste, but I think twice about serving them on a plate with many other foods since they take up quite a lot of room and the dressing is apt to run into other foods. Here is a delicious "buffet" salad.

GOLD AND WHITE SALAD

4-oz. can pimiento, cut in ½″ pieces

½ cup pitted ripe olives, quartered

½ cup stuffed green olives, sliced

3 cups shredded cabbage

1 cup grated carrots

½ medium onion, grated

1 cup shredded iceberg lettuce

1 cup toasted, slivered almonds

3 tbsp. French dressing

1 tbsp. lemon juice

¼ to ½ cup mayonnaise

spinach

endive

Combine first six ingredients and chill in refrigerator. When ready to serve, add lettuce. Toss with French dressing and lemon juice. Add mayonnaise to bind. Line salad bowl with spinach and endive leaves. Put salad into prepared salad bowl. Sprinkle almonds over the top. *6 to 8 servings.*

Molded fruit salads are among the prettiest of party dishes. Here is one I find popular with many of my guests.

SPICED PEACH FRUIT MOLD

no. 303 can Bing cherries
no. 2½ can Cling peach halves
1 tbsp. whole cloves
2 to 3″ stick cinnamon
¼ cup lemon juice
1 pkg. lemon-flavored gelatin
1 pkg. lime-flavored gelatin
1 cup diced, unpeeled apple
½ cup Tokay grapes, halved and seeded
1 orange, peeled and diced
¼ cup broken pecans

Drain cherries. Drain peach halves also but reserve the syrup. Add water to peach syrup to make 1¾ cups. Pour syrup in saucepan with cloves, cinnamon, and lemon juice. Bring to boil, simmer 10 minutes. Add peaches, heat slowly 5 minutes more. Remove peaches from syrup; place cut-side-up in 3-qt. ring mold (11″ diameter). Place an equal number drained cherries between each peach half. Strain syrup; measure and add hot water to make 2 cups. Bring to boil. Add to lemon-flavored gelatin, stirring until dissolved. Pour over peaches. Chill until almost firm. Meanwhile, prepare fruits and pecans. Dissolve lime-flavored gelatin in 1 cup boiling water. Add 8 to 12 ice cubes and stir constantly for 3 minutes, until gelatin starts to thicken. Remove unmelted ice. Let stand about 5 minutes, add fruits and pecans. Pour over peach layer. Chill until firm. Unmold on crisp lettuce or other greens, fill center with greens. Serve with Fruit Salad Mayonnaise (fold ½ cup mayonnaise into ¼ cup whipping cream, whipped). *10 to 12 servings.*

Good breads are important to any meal; hot rolls are a great favorite. It helps to serve them ready-buttered at a buffet. Nearly everyone enjoys garlic bread, but here is a substitute if you are not certain that all of your guests like garlic, or if you are using garlic in some other food.

HERB LOAF

Soften ¼ lb. butter. Cream it with 2 tsp. chopped parsley, ½ tsp. oregano, ⅛ tsp. garlic salt, 2 tbsp. grated Parmesan cheese. Cut a French loaf in slices and spread each slice on both sides with the herb butter. Wrap in foil and heat in moderately hot oven (400°) 10 minutes. Five minutes before serving, open the foil and let the top of the loaf become crusty again.

Everyone is impressed by homemade bread. People seem to have forgotten that our grandmothers did all the family baking as a matter of course. Baking bread does take a little extra time, but it is so very good that it is well worth the effort. Here is a bread recipe, especially easy because it does not require kneading.

ANADAMA BATTER BREAD

¾ cup boiling water
½ cup yellow corn meal
3 tbsp. shortening
¼ cup molasses
2 tsp. salt

¼ cup warm water
  (not hot—110 to 115°)
1 pkg. active dry yeast
1 egg
2¾ cups *sifted* GOLD
  MEDAL Flour

Stir together in a large mixer bowl, boiling water, corn meal, shortening, molasses, salt. Cool to lukewarm. Dissolve yeast in warm water. Add yeast, egg, and half the flour to luke-warm mixture. Beat 2 minutes, medium speed on mixer or 300 vigorous strokes by hand. Scrape sides and bottom of bowl frequently. Add rest of flour and mix with spoon until flour is thoroughly blended into dough. Spread batter evenly in greased loaf pan, 8½ x 4½ x 2¾" or 9 x 5 x 3". Batter will be sticky. Smooth out top of loaf by flouring hand and patting into shape.

Let rise in warm place (85°) until batter reaches top of 8½ x 4½ x 2¾" pan or 1" from top of 9 x 5 x 3" pan—about 1½ hours. Sprinkle top with a little corn meal and salt.

Heat oven to 375° (quick moderate). Bake *50 to 55 minutes.* To test loaf, tap the top crust. It should sound hollow. Crust will be dark brown. Immediately remove bread from pan. Place on a cooling rack or across edges of bread pans. Brush top with melted butter or shortening. Do not place in direct draft. Cool before cutting.

Desserts for buffet dinners must be as carefully chosen as the main dishes so that they cause no major last-minute demands on the hostess, are delightful to look at, and can wait without damage. Here are three different ones that fill those requirements:

CHOCOLATE MERINGUE TORTE
(Pictured on p. 143.)

Heat oven to 275° (slow). Make meringue shells as directed, using 2 packets Betty Crocker Meringue Mix, spreading meringue evenly in four 7½" circles on paper-covered baking sheets. Bake *1 hour*. Turn off oven. Let circles dry in oven for 1 hour. Stack circles together with chocolate filling between, making sure filling is spread to edge. Chill. Cut in wedges to serve. *10 to 12 servings.*

Chocolate Filling: Melt two 6-oz. packages semi-sweet chocolate pieces over hot water. Stir in 1 tbsp. powdered instant coffee and ¼ cup boiling water. Beat until creamy and slightly cool. Fold in 1 cup whipping cream, whipped, and 1 tsp. vanilla.

ICE CREAM POLKA DOT DESSERT

1 qt. chocolate or mocha ice cream
1 qt. pistachio or mint ice cream
1 qt. strawberry ice cream

4 qt. vanilla ice cream
1 pt. whipping cream, whipped
½ tsp. almond flavoring

Chill a 10" tube pan with removable bottom. With a small scoop, shape balls of chocolate, pistachio, and strawberry ice cream. Place on baking sheet and freeze until firm. Soften vanilla ice cream, and whip until like fluffy whipped cream. Drop layer of colored balls into pan. Add whipped ice cream to fill spaces. Repeat until pan is full. Freeze several hours or overnight, until firm. Remove from pan. Frost with whipped cream flavored with almond. Cut in wedges and serve immediately. *18 to 20 servings.*

GAY NINETIES CHARLOTTE RUSSE
(Pictured on p. 142.)

Grease lightly with butter a 1½-qt. ring mold. Line mold with angel food cake. Begin at bottom of mold by placing a small round piece in the center. Cover the rest of the bottom with pieces cut into triangles, placing them close together around the center piece. Place cake strips (1" wide and ½" thick) about 2" apart inside of mold. Fill mold with Vanilla Bavarian Cream.

Vanilla Bavarian Cream

½ cup sugar	4 egg yolks, slightly beaten
1 envelope unflavored gelatin (1 tbsp.)	1 cup whipping cream, whipped
½ tsp. salt	1 tsp. vanilla
2¼ cups milk	

Blend thoroughly in saucepan sugar, gelatin, salt, milk, and egg yolks. Cook over medium heat, stirring constantly, just until mixture comes to a boil. Place pan in cold water; cool until mixture mounds slightly when dropped from a spoon. Fold in whipped cream and vanilla. Pour into mold and chill until firm, 6 to 8 hours or overnight. Unmold on large serving plate. Garnish top and sides with pecans, walnuts, or maraschino cherries. Serve with Apricot Sauce (below) and top with sweetened whipped cream. *8 to 10 servings.*

Apricot Sauce

Wash ½ lb. dried apricots. Simmer in 1 cup water until soft. Put in blender or rub apricots through sieve. Add ½ cup sugar. Cook over medium heat 10 minutes. Stir frequently. Cool.

Coffee comes last. If you are using regular cups, let guests help themselves from a big pot on table or sideboard. For a large group, coffee in demitasses usually is poured into the cups and they are passed by host or hostess on a big tray.

Clearing-up

Dessert plates, coffee cups, and napkins need not be picked up in haste the minute the meal is finished. Indeed, it is more graceful if the hostess does not make a big project of clearing away, but instead, removes plates a few at a time inconspicuously as she moves around offering additional coffee, bonbons, or cigarettes.

With that, the work of the hostess is done—except for washing the dishes.

At every big party I have ever given, without help, some kind guest always says, "Now let's do the dishes. I can't bear to leave you with them. It won't take a minute if we help."

I always refuse, though with warmest appreciation of the thought. I have been away from my guests long enough, no matter how well planned in advance my kitchen duties have been. Now I want to enjoy my company. Also, they have dressed prettily and I do not want a lovely dress spotted with dishwater.

I much prefer to deal with the dishes and to put away the left-over food in calm and quiet alone. Besides, I *like* washing dishes. Crystal, china, and silver is lovely as it comes gleaming out of the water. I enjoy handling these pretty possessions.

Pot Luck Dinners

WHEN I WAS a little girl, my very best friend lived six blocks away. We spent our afternoons after school together, either at her house or at mine. She had five brothers and sisters so dinner at her house always seemed like a party to me, just from sheer numbers.

An invitation I loved, and heard many times from her mother was, "Betty, would you like to stay and take pot luck with us so that you and Jean can finish your game after dinner?"

"I'd love to, if you are sure you'll have enough without a lot of trouble," I always answered eagerly.

"No trouble at all. I'll call your mother and tell her I'm adding a cup of water to the soup," was her usual smiling reply.

Her soup was never anything but thick and savory, but for years, I took her literally. I truly believed that those dinners which expanded so miraculously to include me and often one or two other extra youngsters were straight from the water tap.

Looking back, I realize how good a lesson she was in hospitality, and how well she made good her claim, "Always enough here for one more we love."

Here are some of the hints she gave me, long after, when I had the vision to ask her exactly how she had stretched her meals so often and with such seeming ease.

"The big secret is having a few packaged and canned or frozen things in reserve that can be added quickly to other dishes in such a way that nothing looks skimpy," she said. "For instance, a stew for four divided among five looks, and is, meager. But take that same stew, add a can of whole boiled onions and a few fresh carrots, whip up some fluffy dumplings or crown it with biscuits in a big casserole, and your main dish looks like a feast, and also is plenty for everyone."

Of course the wise hostess does not issue an invitation to share pot luck unless she has made a quick survey of what she has on the shelves as well as the range, and is sure that she can make additions that will make the guest feel at home. The guest who accepts a last-minute invitation, and sits down to a succulent chop, baked potato or corn on the cob, and a molded individual salad, and sees a fried egg, and no vegetables or salad in front of his hostess cannot feel anything but acute embarrassment.

There is no way to make four chops serve five or six people unless there is time to turn them into a goulash. In such case, it is better not to issue that last minute invitation.

On the other hand, many foods planned for individual servings can be expanded with hardly more than a twist of the wrist.

Four ears of corn and just enough string beans or peas for four are no problem if there is a can of tomatoes in reserve. Cut the corn off the cob, mix it with the green vegetable and the tomatoes, and serve a dish that may be more tasty than the same vegetable served separately—and hospitality is a spice in itself!

Four baked potatoes can be stretched to serve six by splitting them, mixing the steaming interiors with butter, cream, and

seasonings, heaping six of the half-shells, sprinkling with grated cheese and running them under the broiler to toast while a big pan of corn bread, for further expansion of solid food, bakes.

If there is plenty to eat at the main course, there is nothing amiss with offering a choice of two desserts if there isn't time to whip up enough of one to go around.

For instance, if you have just enough tarts, éclairs, or individual servings of pudding for the family, set them forth. Add a bowl of canned fruit, some cookies, cake, or whatever you can find, and let guests make first choice.

Don't forget instant puddings for this emergency. Those that are made by adding powdered ingredients to cold milk, whipping briefly, and pouring into separate custard cups can be ready in five minutes. These take on a real party air if a tablespoonful of strawberry preserves, orange marmalade, or raspberry jam is put in the bottom of each cup. A canned peach or apricot half, or crumbled macaroons, are good additions. Chopped nuts are a good quick topping if you have no whipping cream. A crumbled toasted cooky will serve the same purpose. It is better to make do with what is in the kitchen than to risk making your guest uneasy and apologetic by whisking someone off to the store for any supply.

Last-minute hospitality is much easier, and very much more impressive, if you have one special shelf stocked for just such a demand so that you can say confidently, "Do stay—there is plenty."

Last year I was asked to speak to a group of June brides about this very matter. Following is a list of "Emergency Rations" I recommended to them. With these in reserve, last-minute dinners may be whipped together with no scurrying to the delicatessen.

This list is designed to supplement shelves stocked with the staples always on hand in any kitchen such as flour, sugar, coffee, and a refrigerator with the normal supply of butter, milk, eggs, and lettuce in it. It could be expanded very sizably, of course, but with even this small reserve stock, a very large variety of tempting menus can be assembled. I asked my June brides to see how many tasty emergency meals they could design from it. In half an hour, one girl listed two dozen quite different ones!

A word of counsel! Well-stocked shelves do not work miracles all by themselves. The important thing about any "Emergency Ration" list is to make it a collection of things you know exactly when, and in what combinations, to use. Read my list. Cut out some items and substitute others of your choice, with several menus firmly in mind. Here is just one example of a complete dinner of reserve supplies, with nothing fresh except the lettuce—even the coffee cream came powdered out of a jar!

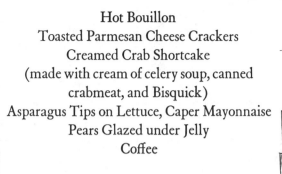

Hot Bouillon
Toasted Parmesan Cheese Crackers
Creamed Crab Shortcake
(made with cream of celery soup, canned
crabmeat, and Bisquick)
Asparagus Tips on Lettuce, Caper Mayonnaise
Pears Glazed under Jelly
Coffee

It is so easy to make dream dinners in your mind! And so easy for the clever hostess to give them, once she charts her course! Don't be satisfied to plan menus and stock shelves. It is much wiser to take a trial run! Some Sunday night, treat your entire family like Pot Luck guests. Pull a whole meal off the shelf, and see how it works. Time yourself, so you know exactly what you need to do when you issue that always welcome invitation, "Let's have dinner at our place—it's in the house."

For Your Emergency Shelf

Soups, canned
  cream of chicken
  cream of celery
  tomato
  black bean
  consommé, canned
    or in cubes
Meats and fish, canned
  salmon

crab or lobster
chicken
ham
Vegetables, canned
  tomatoes, whole pack
  onions, whole
  corn
  asparagus
  mushrooms

beets
beans: Lima, kidney,
   chili, and baked
Starches
   potatoes, instant mashed
   rice
   spaghetti, macaroni, noodles
Breads
   biscuit mix
   pancake mix
   corn bread mix
   muffin mix
   crackers
Desserts
   puddings, instant
   cake mix
   frosting mix
   pie crust mix

cookie mix
gingerbread mix
peach halves, canned
apricot halves, canned
pear halves, canned
cherries, canned
Miscellaneous, canned
or in glass
   anchovies
   pimientos
   black olives
   milk, evaporated
   cream, powdered
   mayonnaise
   nuts
   spaghetti sauce
   Parmesan cheese, grated
   lemon juice

"Come by for Dessert and Coffee"

Entertaining after dinner is growing fast in popularity. It is an especially pleasant and practical plan for hostesses who hold day-time jobs or have very small children who need to be bathed, fed, and put to sleep in the earlier part of the evening.

It also is the most convenient way to entertain for those living in extremely small quarters, such as a young couple I know.

He is a divinity student. She is working as a secretary until he gets his degree. They have wisely put current comfort second to ambition for their future, and are living in a one-room apartment.

It has a tiny range and sink behind a Venetian blind. She is an excellent cook, but obviously cannot ask more than one couple for dinner. There is no place to put used dishes for more.

"But we can take care of ten after dinner—and without the range and sink staring at us," she said. "And we find that many of our friends like the idea of an after-dinner get-together as much as we do. Some with babies like to put them to sleep rather than let a baby-sitter do it, so they much prefer to join us around nine o'clock when everything at home is under control."

This young friend makes a point of choosing a dessert that is dainty in appearance but fairly substantial, such as a warm fruit pie à la mode, a chiffon cheese cake, or an elaborate layer cake. One with an exceptionally good filling starts with our White Cake Mix and Fluffy White Frosting Mix. She bakes it the night before her party. When the layers are cool she spreads in this filling:

MAGGIE'S BUTTER-NUT CAKE FILLING

Mix ½ cup sugar, 1 tbsp. flour, 3 tbsp. orange juice, ½ cup soft butter, ¼ cup chopped dates or raisins in saucepan, and cook over low heat, stirring until mixture boils. Boil 1 minute. Pour half into 2 egg yolks, beaten, stirring constantly, then stir into filling remaining in saucepan. Bring to a boil. Add ½ cup chopped nuts. Cool before filling cake. *Makes 1¼ cups.*

She spreads the frosting on in big swirls later in the evening, and is all ready to serve it the following night from her small drop-leaf table flanked by coffee cups, sugar, cream, and an electric percolator—with the Venetian blind firmly lowered in front of her cooking facilities.

Éclairs are a good choice, also, since they may be baked the night before, and the chilled filling added just before guests arrive. Better allow two to a guest, though. They are popular.

FRENCH SILK CHOCOLATE PUFFS

1 stick Betty Crocker
 Cream Puff Mix
¾ cup soft butter
1 cup sugar
1½ tsp. vanilla

1½ tsp. powdered instant
 coffee
3 eggs
3 sq. unsweetened
 chocolate (3-oz.),
 melted and cooled

Heat oven to 425° (hot). Follow directions on package for 8 medium-sized puffs. Cream butter and sugar together on mixer. Blend in vanilla and coffee. Add eggs one at a time, beating 2 minutes after each addition. Blend in chocolate. Chill for at least 1 hour. Fill puffs and sprinkle with confectioners' sugar. Both filling and puffs can be made ahead. Put filling in puffs just before serving.

Guests usually leave at about the same time they would after dinner, or slightly later—about eleven, and certainly by midnight. If a later party had been planned, invitations would have been to "drop in after dinner," which is a tacit promise of refreshment to be served much later in the evening.

Midnight Suppers

"COME AROUND NINE," is a welcome invitation I hear with increasing frequency from friends who like to bring ten to twenty or more friends together on a Friday or Saturday night, but who do not have the time, stamina, money, or inclination to cook, serve, and clean up after a dinner party for that many.

I always look forward with pleasure to such a party.

It is much easier on the hostess than a buffet dinner, and more comfortable for many guests, also, since this is one invitation involving a meal that does not require appearing right on the dot.

Saturday often is a busy day for the man of the house. Gardening, golfing, assisting with shopping, puttering with screen or storm doors, and a dozen other pleasures and chores usually are concentrated in this one afternoon.

A dinner date at seven means that he must drop everything around five to shower, dress, get the car or other transportation, and be on the way. The same is true of the mother who is going to a matinee, taking children

to the beach or dancing class, and getting youngsters fed and settled for the evening. Arriving on time for dinner, when there are young children in the house, often means a frantic unpartylike rush for everyone—including the hostess.

"We love to dress up a little when we go out," a young wife explained. "And it's so much easier to slip into a party dress after dinner at home than to rush around cooking for the children and the baby-sitter, shower, dress, and leave the house by six-thirty. We feel more relaxed and party-spirited drifting in whenever we can make it easily after nine."

Often the party starting at nine has some definite plan. Perhaps it is a late television show, some new records, dancing, cards, or other games. If so, the hostess usually says so when she issues her invitations. If guests agree to complete a bridge table, they should arrive reasonably soon after nine; and it is not thoughtful to arrive after a television show, mentioned in an invitation, has started. Otherwise, it is proper to arrive any time before ten. If you are going to be very much later, it is kind to explain, "We have theater tickets for that evening, so we can't reach you until eleven-thirty or so. Is that all right?" This leaves the hostess sure of the number she is going to serve, rather than wondering all evening if you have forgotten the date or met with some mischance.

Supper is served any time after midnight.

One of the simplest, and a very attractive one, is a generously stocked cheese board, a lovely cake, coffee, and tea. The effectiveness of this depends on offering a sizable variety of cheeses with a certain amount of drama. A big hardwood cheese board is ideal. A large chop plate or tray also looks well. Most cheeses may be kept indefinitely, properly wrapped, in the refrigerator. So let yourself go, and buy plenty of quite a number of different kinds. Nothing looks quite so meager as a meager cheese board.

A wedge of Roquefort or Bleu will please those who like very sharp cheeses. For those who enjoy the mild ones, add Brie, Bel Paese, or in California, their magnificent Jack cheese so delicate that it is rarely exported. A soft wheel of Camembert and a ball of red Edam are festive. A block of pale gold Swiss, another of stout yellow Cheddar, a stick of smoked cheese in its tempting brown rind, Sage, Caraway—the choice is almost endless.

With the cheese, all you need are baskets of crackers, and plenty of rye, pumpernickel, or other firm rich breads.

This is finger food, requiring no plates. If you want to make things really easy for yourself, serve a white or dark fruitcake, or a close-grained pound cake made with our mix, of either the golden or the marble. Then all you need are cups, saucers, and spoons for tea and coffee, or hot chocolate and the midnight supper is yours to share and enjoy.

REMEMBRANCE FRUITCAKE
(Pictured on p. 34.)

1 cup cooking (salad) oil
1½ cups sugar
4 eggs
3 cups *sifted*
   GOLD MEDAL Flour
1 tsp. baking powder
2 tsp. salt
1 cup pineapple or
   apple juice
1 cup thinly sliced citron

½ cup thinly sliced
   candied lemon peel
1 cup candied pineapple
   (in 1" pieces)
1½ cups whole candied
   cherries
3 cups (1 lb.) seedless
   white raisins
2 cups nuts in
   large pieces

Heat oven to 275° (slow). Line with brown paper 2 greased loaf pans, 8½ x 4½ x 2¾". Mix oil, sugar, eggs, and beat vigorously with spoon or electric mixer 2 minutes. Sift together 2 cups of the flour, baking powder, salt. Stir in oil mixture alternately with pineapple juice. Mix fruits and nuts with third cup of flour. Pour batter over floured fruit, mixing thoroughly. Pour into pans. Bake *2½ to 3 hours.* After baking, let cakes stand 15 minutes before removing from pans. Cool thoroughly on racks without removing paper. When cool, remove paper, wrap, and store to ripen in cool dry place. *Makes two 3-lb. loaves.*

One hot dish with hot rolls, cake, coffee, and tea is easy to prepare though you will have more dishes to deal with later. Good choices are light casseroles, such as creamed sea foods, sweetbreads, ham, chipped beef, chicken à la king, and curried eggs.

Toast for a large group takes too much last minute attention. Get patty shells from the baker or make cream puffs from our mix and keep them crisp in the oven until ready to fill. Rice can be cooked in advance and kept warm in a double boiler. Or make buttercups by brushing thinly sliced bread (crusts removed) with melted butter, pressing them into muffin cups and toasting in a moderate oven (350°).

A pasta dish—lasagne, ravioli, or gnocchi in a rich spanish sauce —or turkey Tetrazzini is also a tempting possibility.

TURKEY AND HAM TETRAZZINI

7 oz. spaghetti
¼ cup butter
¼ cup **GOLD MEDAL** Flour
1 tsp. salt
¼ tsp. white pepper
¼ tsp. nutmeg
2 cups chicken or turkey broth or 14½-oz. can chicken broth
1 cup rich milk
3 tbsp. sherry flavoring
2 cups cooked turkey, cut in small pieces

½ cup cooked cubed ham
¼ cup chopped green pepper, sautéed *or* 4-oz. can pimiento, cut up
1 cup ripe olives, cut in large pieces *or* ½ lb. mushrooms, sliced and sautéed in butter 5 minutes
1 egg yolk
½ cup grated Parmesan cheese *or* ½ cup slivered toasted almonds

Heat oven to 350° (moderate). Break spaghetti in about 2″ pieces and drop into 6 cups rapidly boiling salted water (4 tsp. salt). Bring back to rapid boil. Cook, stirring constantly 3 minutes. Cover with tight-fitting lid. Remove from heat, let stand 10 minutes. Rinse with hot water and drain.

Melt butter over low heat in heavy saucepan. Blend in flour and seasonings. Cook over low heat, stirring until mixture is smooth and bubbly. Remove from heat. Stir in broth and milk. Bring to boil; boil 1 minute, stirring constantly. Blend in sherry flavoring. Add sauce to cooked spaghetti. Add turkey, ham, green pepper, olives, and egg yolk to spaghetti. Pour into 2-qt. baking dish. Sprinkle with cheese or almonds. Bake uncovered *25 to 30 minutes*. Let stand 10 minutes before serving. *6 to 8 servings.*

Delicate enchiladas or chicken crêpes can be prepared in advance and heated in a shallow oven-proof serving dish under their rich sauce just before needed. So can small individual pizzas if English muffins are used for the base of bland Italian cheese, tomato paste, bits of anchovy or spicy sausage, and the sprinkling of thyme or oregano that gives this hearty dainty its characteristic flavor. A Welsh rarebit, kept warm in a double boiler, is another enormously popular late-evening dish, and easy to bring out whenever needed if English muffins are kept warm (rather than toasted at the last minute) to be covered with this smooth, rich cheese sauce just before serving.

Cake, torte, chiffon pie, cream puffs, petits fours, or candy-like cookies can follow depending on your choice of main dish and the appetites of your friends.

Here are three different desserts that are very good by themselves and also delightful with ice cream.

LEMON COCONUT CAKE

¼ cup lemon juice
15-oz. can sweetened
   condensed milk
2 tsp. grated lemon rind

Betty Crocker Angel
   Food Cake
   (baked as directed on
   package)
½ cup finely chopped
   coconut, toasted

Add lemon juice slowly to condensed milk. Stir until thickened. Add grated lemon rind. Chill 30 minutes. Cut angel food cake in 3 layers. Spread about ⅓ cup of lemon mixture between each layer. Spread remaining mixture on top and sides. Sprinkle top with coconut.

BROWNIE PEPPERMINT PIE

Heat oven to 350° (moderate). Prepare 1 package of our Betty Crocker Brownie Mix and pour into a greased 9″ round layer pan. Bake *10 minutes*. While pie is baking melt 2 sq. unsweetened chocolate (2 oz.) and add ¼ tsp. peppermint extract. Take pie from oven and quickly drizzle chocolate mixture on top. Bake *15 to 20 minutes more*. When cool, cut in wedges and top with ice cream. *8 to 10 servings*.

WHEATIES NOUGAT BARS

3 tbsp. butter
½ lb. marshmallows
4 cups Wheaties
½ cup coarsely chopped nuts
½ cup moist shredded coconut
½ tsp. salt
4 sq. sweet or semi-sweet chocolate (4-oz.), melted

Melt butter and marshmallows over hot water, stirring occasionally. Take from heat. Fold in Wheaties, nuts, coconut, and salt. Pat mixture evenly in buttered 8 or 9″ square pan. Pour melted chocolate over top and spread evenly. Chill about 1 hour. *Makes 32 bars*.

Late suppers are most easily and gracefully set out in a dining room or on a buffet so that guests can help themselves, or each other. Part of the charm of this form of entertaining is its informality. The hostess does well to help and deliver plates to any small group that seems to be entirely absorbed in a discussion, but many groups may welcome the chance to break up and mingle with others. An invitation to help one's self may be just the opportunity an anchored guest needs for a change of pace.

The serving of a late supper usually marks the end of the party. Guests may start for home as soon as they have had some of the refreshment, or within about half an hour as an expected limit.

Stag Parties

EVEN IF THE hostess does not appear at all on an evening that the man of the house is devoting to his male friends—either for cards, a club meeting, or a conference—her hospitality is happily evident if refreshments are planned and prepared in advance.

Quite often the hostess is briefly on hand to welcome her husband's friends as they gather early in the evening. Just as often, a wife leaves early for a visit in the neighborhood or a movie. In either case, the evening is off to a good start if simple, hearty, and easy-to-serve refreshments are waiting for the men to find for themselves when they are ready. The whole idea of a stag party is "No women!" So it is better to leave behind you simpler fare than to stir around the edges of such a party concocting a feast.

Men like the idea that they are foraging for themselves. They can still have the fun of raiding the refrigerator, but without confusion, if plates, napkins, silver, mustard, relishes, and anything else that can wait without damage are set out on a sideboard or table. A baked ham, a big wedge of cheese under a cover, a loaf of rye bread, and a cake, with proper knives ready for carving and cutting, is a sensible choice. So is a chicken or veal loaf, or a platter of cold cuts with olives, stuffed eggs, and pickles.

The makings of hero or poor-boy sandwiches, assembled on one or two big serving plates ready to be lifted out of the refrigerator is another: sliced salami, tomatoes, onion rings, cucumber, mild dill pickles, small green chilies, and crusty French bread for a start.

A well-seasoned homemade potato salad is popular. Here is a recipe that produces a truly savory one.

GOURMET POTATO SALAD

3 cups cubed cold boiled
   potatoes
1 tbsp. finely chopped
   onion
diced whites from 2 large
   hard-cooked eggs
½ tsp. salt
dash of pepper

mashed yolks from
   2 hard-cooked eggs
⅔ cup commercial
   sour cream
2 tbsp. vinegar
1 tsp. prepared mustard
½ tsp. celery seeds
2 tbsp. mayonnaise
⅓ cup sweet relish

Place in bowl potatoes, onion, and egg whites. Sprinkle with salt and pepper. Mix remaining ingredients and pour over potato mixture and toss lightly. *6 servings.*

One hot dish is an especially good thought for a winter night. A big pot of home-baked beans, rich with salt pork and brown sugar, can stay safely in a warming oven all evening; and it is hard to beat a big casserole of chili. Here is a recipe for one I like:

SPICY CHILI

1 lb. ground beef
1 large onion, sliced
1 green pepper, chopped
no. 2½ can tomatoes
   (3½ cups)
3 whole cloves
1 large or 2 small
   bay leaves

1 to 2 tbsp. chili powder
½ stick cinnamon
1½ tsp. salt
⅛ tsp. cayenne pepper
⅛ tsp. paprika
no. 2 can kidney beans

Crumble and brown ground beef in heavy skillet (no fat added). Add onion and green pepper; cook until almost tender. Add tomatoes and seasonings. Cover. Simmer gently 2 hours, adding liquid from kidney beans and water a little at a time, if needed, to keep at desired consistency. Add kidney beans; heat through. Remove bay leaves. Serve in small bowls. *6 servings*.

Most men have a weakness for chocolate cake. So do women and children, for that matter! Here is one of the best I have ever eaten.

"LOVELIGHT" CHOCOLATE CHIFFON CAKE

2 eggs, separated
1½ cups sugar
1¾ cups *sifted*
  SOFTASILK Cake Flour
¾ tsp. soda
1 tsp. salt

⅓ cup cooking (salad) oil
1 cup buttermilk
  or sweet milk
2 sq. unsweetened
  chocolate (2 oz.),
  melted

Heat oven to 350° (moderate). Grease generously and dust with flour 2 round layer pans, 8″ by at least 1½″ deep, or 9 x 1½″, or one oblong pan, 13 x 9½ x 2″.

Beat egg whites until frothy. Gradually beat in ½ cup of the sugar. Continue beating until very stiff and glossy.

Sift remaining sugar, flour, soda, salt into another bowl. Add oil, half of buttermilk. Beat 1 minute, medium speed on mixer or 150 vigorous strokes by hand. Scrape sides and bottom of bowl constantly. Add remaining buttermilk, egg yolks, chocolate. Beat 1 more minute, scraping bowl constantly. Fold in meringue. Pour into prepared pans. Bake layers 30 to 35 minutes; oblong 40 to 45 minutes. Cool. Ice with White Mountain Icing (recipe below) or our Fluffy White Frosting Mix. Sprinkle with coconut.

WHITE MOUNTAIN ICING

Mix in saucepan ½ cup sugar, 2 tbsp. water, and ¼ cup light corn syrup. Cover saucepan, bring to rolling boil. Remove cover and cook to 242° or until syrup spins a 6 to 8″ thread. Just before syrup is ready, beat 2 egg whites (¼ cup) until stiff enough to hold a point. Pour hot syrup very slowly in a thin stream into the beaten egg whites. Continue to beat until frosting holds peaks. Blend in 1 tsp. vanilla.

CHOCOLATE CREAM "LOVELIGHT" CAKE

Make cake according to recipe above. When cool, split each layer into two layers. Spread Chocolate Fluff between layers and over cake. Store in refrigerator until used.

Chocolate Fluff: Mix in chilled bowl 2 cups chilled whipping cream, 1 cup *sifted* confectioners' sugar, ½ cup cocoa, dash of salt. Beat until stiff enough to hold a point.

Lunches

"CAN YOU HAVE lunch with me this week? I'm giving my first big luncheon next month and I have a thousand questions," a bride said to me recently. "And the first one is when to say 'lunch,' and when to say 'luncheon'?" she added.

This is a matter that confuses many people.

I don't think it makes a great deal of difference. However, "Come to lunch" is considered better usage in either spoken or written invitations.

The word 'luncheon,' is used properly to describe a large party, formal to some degree. An example: "The Board is giving an anniversary luncheon for the minister," or "Joyce is introducing her new sister-in-law at a luncheon at the country club." Even so, invitations to a party big and formal enough to be termed a "luncheon" are best phrased "come to lunch," since many people feel that "come to luncheon" sounds slightly affected or pretentious.

An invitation to lunch means that guests are expected to arrive promptly at the time mentioned, and leave about an hour after the meal is finished unless the hostess adds a specific invitation to stay longer, such as "Lunch at one, and bridge later," or "Lunch at twelve-thirty, and the rest of the afternoon sewing for the Red Cross."

Table settings and decorations for lunch have their own special attractions and opportunities. No matter how formal a lunch may be, the table is set somewhat less formally than for a dinner party.

Mats, runners, or the smaller tablecloths are preferred to great sweeping damask cloths. These may be of colored cotton, rough peasant linen, intricate cut-work, or delicately embroidered organdy, just so long as they are in keeping with the rest of the table setting.

It looks a little strange to see heavy pottery plates, colorful and charming as they are, on exquisite lace-edged mats. Water glasses are chosen to match china in mood—fragile crystal with fine thin china, simpler glassware with a pottery service.

Flat silver is the exception to this rule. Knives and forks with novelty bone or wooden handles are suitable for a meal served on heavy chinaware or pottery, but it is entirely proper to use sterling flatware at any meal, from a backyard barbecue served on paper plates to the most formal of dinners.

Standard-sized napkins, matching the table cloth in mood, rather than over-sized damask ones are the best choice for lunch.

A midweek lunch usually is a party for women. Week end lunch parties for both men and women are growing fast in popularity, though these often are called brunch, and are rather more akin to lunch than to the midday Sunday dinner that was a standard social event for our grandparents.

If there are men present, the hostess seats her guests just as she would at a dinner party. If the party is for women only, the hostess leads the way to her dining room, or serving area, and directs the guest of honor, if there is one, to the place at her right. If she wishes, she indicates to other guests where she would like them to sit. Rather more often guests find their own places.

If lunch is just the start of an afternoon of companionship, the wise hostess cooks dinner for the family in advance, as well, so that at the end of a long gay day she does not find herself back over a hot range for any length of time.

When guests are invited for an early lunch and the rest of the afternoon, lemonade, a fruit punch, iced tea, or some other simple thirst quencher is often offered at three-thirty or four o'clock, though this is in no way necessary. (Suggestions for such beverages are found in the chapter devoted to teas.) No food is offered with them. Hot coffee or tea is not served in the late afternoon following a lunch party—otherwise the effect is of two parties rather than one.

Little children are best handed over to a baby sitter or dispatched for the middle of the day to grandmother's when a big lunch party is under way. During the summer when older children are home from school, a carefully worked out schedule for them is first on the list of any wise and wary hostess. You might send them to the drugstore for sandwiches and milk shakes, and then to the movies or playground if such diversions are easily reached, or plan something that will keep them diverted and out from under foot.

Candles are not used on a lunch table, except on a dark day, so it is doubly important to plan some imaginative centerpiece. A low bowl of flowers is always attractive, but decorations that are a conversation piece are more fun.

One of my friends with two girls, 10 and 12, and a boy of 9, makes an event of a special meal for them to enjoy by themselves or with guests of their own when she is giving a lunch party.

During the morning she packs a picnic basket or separate box lunches that the children can carry to the park. They think this is a fine adventure because their mother dramatizes their responsibility for themselves during her party.

There is a wide choice of foods that seem especially attractive and suitable for lunch, whether it is a one-plate meal on porch or patio or a three-course party in your dining room. In general, these are more delicate dishes than you would choose for dinner.

First Courses

Appetizers usually are not offered before lunch. If you are planning a three-course lunch for a large group, the safest choice is a first course that can be in place on the table before guests arrive, such as a jellied Madrilene, vichyssoise, or a fruit cocktail. However, two of the most novel hot soups I know are unusually good at lunch. They are well worth the time it takes to pour into soup cups since they never fail to produce demands for the recipes— which I think is the prettiest of compliments.

CREAM OF ALMOND SOUP

1 tbsp. butter or margarine
1 tbsp. flour
¾ tsp. salt
⅛ tsp. pepper
1½ to 2 cups chicken
  stock or consommé

¾ cup finely chopped,
  toasted almonds
2 cups cream
grated rind of 1 lemon
paprika

Melt butter over low heat. Blend in flour, salt, and pepper. Cook over low heat, stirring until mixture is smooth and bubbly. Remove from heat. Add chicken stock and almonds. Boil 1 minute, stirring constantly. Add cream. Heat through; do not boil. Serve sprinkled with lemon rind and paprika. *4 to 6 servings. Or 8 to 10 very small servings.*

Much more filling and somewhat more emphatic in flavor is a cheese soup that is wonderfully good on a cold snowy day. It was just such a day in Ontario when I first tasted this.

CANADIAN CHEESE SOUP
(Pictured on p. 137.)

1 large potato, finely
  diced
1 large onion, finely
  chopped
¼ cup finely diced
  carrots
¼ cup finely diced celery

1 cup water
no. 303 can chicken broth
  (about 2 cups)
1 cup grated sharp Cheddar
  cheese (¼ lb.)
½ cup cream
2 tbsp. chopped parsley

In covered saucepan, simmer vegetables in water until tender, 10 to 15 minutes. Add remaining ingredients except parsley. Heat and serve garnished with parsley. *4 to 6 servings.*

Soup at lunch, either thick or thin, is served in soup cups rather than in soup plates. Hearty meal-in-themselves soups such as bouillabaisse or thick chowder containing pieces of potato, fish, or clams are usually served at the table from a tureen, and in big soup plates.

A two-course lunch is the best choice for the hostess serving without help of a maid, I find. She concentrates on an excellent main course and a lovely dessert, and avoids interruption of conversation while she changes first course plates.

Good hot lunch dishes are rissoto with ham, shrimp, and chicken, golden and savory with saffron and other herbs, an eggplant casserole bubbling under tomato and cheese, or any of the hot dishes in the chapter on Midnight Suppers. An excellent casserole is:

SHRIMP DE JONGHE
(Pictured on p. 33.)

2 lb. cleaned cooked, shelled shrimp
4 to 5 cloves garlic, sliced
1 cup butter
¼ tsp. tarragon
¼ tsp. minced parsley
¼ tsp. shallot
¼ tsp. minced onion
dash *each* of nutmeg, mace, thyme
2 tsp. salt
¼ tsp. pepper
½ cup consommé or cooking sherry
1 cup dry bread crumbs

Heat oven to 400° (moderately hot). Place shrimp in 8 individual baking dishes. Cook garlic in butter until butter browns; remove garlic. Add herbs, seasonings, and consommé to butter. Remove ¼ cup butter mixture and toss with bread crumbs. Pour remaining butter mixture over shrimp. Top with buttered crumbs. Bake *15 minutes*. Note: If shallots are not obtainable, increase minced onion to ½ tsp.

An elaborate sandwich loaf has endless variations. Here is a combination I find especially appetizing and attractive.

ELEGANT SANDWICH LOAF
(Pictured on p. 139.)

Trim crusts from an unsliced loaf of sandwich bread, and cut the loaf into four lengthwise slices. Spread one side of each slice with softened and whipped butter (you will need about ½ cup). Place one slice, buttered-side-up, on a serving platter and spread with *Shrimp Salad Filling:* 1 hard-cooked egg, chopped, 1⅓ cups (7-oz. can) chopped shrimp, ¼ cup minced celery, 2 tbsp. lemon juice, ¼ tsp. salt, dash of pepper, ¼ cup mayonnaise, well mixed.

Top with second buttered bread slice and spread it with *Cheese—Pecan Filling:* 3-oz. package cream cheese, softened, 1 cup finely chopped pecans, ¾ cup (9-oz. can) well-drained crushed pineapple, well mixed.

Top with third buttered bread slice and spread with *Chicken-Bacon Filling:* 8 slices crisp bacon, crumbled, 1 cup finely chopped cooked chicken, ¼ cup mayonnaise, 1 tbsp. finely chopped pimiento, ¼ tsp. salt, ⅛ tsp. pepper, well mixed.

Top with remaining bread slice and coat the top and sides of the loaf with the following:
Frosting: Mix two 8-oz. pkg. cream cheese and ½ cup cream well. Add food coloring for a delicate green. Garnish center of loaf with paper-thin slices of unpeeled cucumber; overlap slices entire length. Chill in refrigerator 3 hours or more. Serve cold. *12 to 14 servings.*

On a warm day, a cold mousse of salmon, turkey, or tuna, or a jellied chicken loaf is a pretty and tempting sight on a big platter in front of the hostess.

One of my favorite lunch dishes is a most interesting and savory variation of the always popular chicken pie that I have kept on my star list since I first tasted it several years ago.

IRENE'S CHICKEN PIE TOPPED WITH SAVORY PASTRY

½ lb. sausage meat
12 large mushroom caps, chopped
¼ cup butter
¼ cup flour
1 tsp. salt
¼ tsp. pepper
2 cups chicken stock
⅔ cup cream
2 cups cut-up cooked chicken

Heat oven to 425° (hot). Shape sausage in tiny balls. Sauté balls, remove, drain off fat. Then sauté mushroom caps in a little butter. Melt butter, blend in flour and seasonings. Add chicken stock and cream. Bring to a boil, stirring constantly. Boil 1 minute. Divide chicken, mushrooms, and sausage balls among 6 individual baking dishes. Pour on hot sauce. Top with Savory Pastry (recipe below).

Savory Pastry: Cut ⅓ cup shortening into 1 cup *sifted* GOLD MEDAL Flour and ½ tsp. salt. Add 1 tsp. celery seeds, ½ tsp. paprika, and 2 tbsp. water. Mix well with fork until dough clings together. Round into smooth ball and roll pastry fairly thin on well floured cloth-covered board. Cut in circles the size of each baking dish. Bake *35 to 40 minutes. 6 servings.*

Such hot dishes are pleasantly accompanied by either a green salad or one vegetable, either hot or cold, such as asparagus tips or braised celery, but they need no more than sliced tomatoes or cucumbers and radishes, and something special in the way of hot or cold bread, and a dessert.

Bread is an important feature of all lunches, formal and informal. If you have room on the table, use bread and butter plates. Butter may be put on each little plate before lunch is announced, but bread is not served in advance. It is passed in a basket or bread tray after guests are seated. Additional butter should be at hand to be passed when needed. Cold breads are cut in half slices.

If you choose to serve cold breads, several different kinds may be offered attractively arranged in one bread basket. A good choice might be a dark pumpernickel, a golden nut loaf, some fine-grained white bread, and a flavorsome herb loaf. The latter is a novelty to many people, and easy to make.

Muffins and corn sticks made from a mix, all of the great variety of hot rolls, and hot biscuits are welcome choices for lunch. For parties, I like to add something special to the basic recipes, such as blueberries or raisins in muffins or make them easily with our mixes.

HERB BATTER BREAD
(Pictured on p. 137.)

1¼ cups warm water
(not hot—110 to 115°)

1 pkg. active dry yeast
2 tbsp. soft shortening
2 tsp. salt
2 tbsp. sugar

3 cups *sifted* GOLD
MEDAL Flour

½ tsp. nutmeg
1 tsp. sage
2 tsp. caraway seeds

In mixer bowl, dissolve yeast in warm water. Add shortening, salt, sugar, and half the flour. Beat 2 minutes, medium mixer speed or 300 hand strokes. Scrape sides and bottom of bowl frequently. Add remaining flour, nutmeg, sage, caraway seeds, and blend with spoon until smooth. Scrape batter from sides of bowl. Cover with cloth and let rise in a warm place (85°) until double (about 30 minutes). If kitchen is cold, place dough on rack over bowl of hot water and cover completely.

Beat about 25 strokes. Spread sticky batter evenly in greased loaf pan, 8½ x 4½ x 2¾" or 9 x 5 x 3". Pat top of loaf into shape with floured hand.

Let rise until batter reaches ¼" from top of 8½ x 4½ x 2¾" pan or 1" from top of 9 x 5 x 3" pan (about 40 minutes).

Heat oven to 375° (quick moderate). Bake *45 to 50 minutes*, or until brown. To test, tap top crust; it should sound hollow. Immediately remove from pan. Place on cooling rack or across bread pans. Brush top with melted butter or shortening. Do not place in direct draft. Cool. To make individual loaves, follow recipe above—except divide batter into 6 miniature greased loaf pans, 4¾ x 2⅝ x 1½". Bake *30 to 35 minutes*.

Lunch desserts usually are lighter and somewhat less fancy than those chosen for dinner. Fruit compote, small fruit tarts, chiffon pies, light puddings, fluffy gelatins, sherbet served with small dainty

If you encourage smoking at the table, have a tiny glass or silver ash tray at each place and the smallest of pretty matchbooks. Two cigarettes may be laid on each ash tray, or small open containers may be within easy reach of several guests.

cookies are good choices. The rich, elaborate Charlotte Russes and the more complicated iced cakes usually are reserved for later in the day, but local custom and the appetites of your guests are the best guide. A delightful cake combined with fresh strawberries or any other berries in season is one I like to serve at lunch; it is one of the most striking as well as one of the most delicate and tempting final courses for either lunch or dinner.

BERRY BASKET CAKE

(Pictured on p. 143.)

Bake cake in 9″ layer pans as directed on package of Betty Crocker Yellow or White Cake Mix. Put one baked layer on a baking sheet. *Heat oven to 375°* (quick moderate). Make pie meringue as directed on Betty Crocker Meringue Mix packet. Pile mounds of meringue around the top edge of the cake for a basket effect. Bake *15 to 20 minutes,* until delicately browned. Serve warm or cold with fresh, sweetened berries heaped in the center. Save the plain layer for another meal. *6 to 8 servings.*

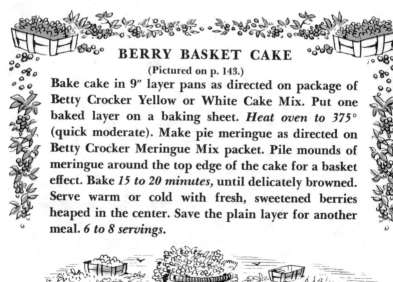

The way to a man's heart is through his stomach!

FRUIT CROWN RING
(Pictured on p. 142.)

1 stick Betty Crocker
  Cream Puff Mix
1½ qt. vanilla ice cream

16-oz. package frozen
fruit (or 1 qt.
fresh fruit)

Heat oven to 425° (hot). Follow directions on package for 1 stick mix. Spoon dough into an 8 or 9″ greased ring mold. Bake *30 to 35 minutes.* Cool. Remove ring from pan to serving plate. Fill center with ice cream. Top with fruit and serve immediately.

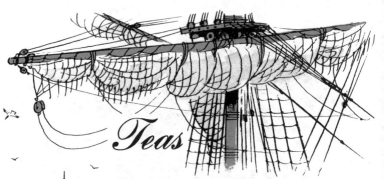

Teas

AFTERNOON TEAS are most generally parties for women, though it is pleasant to see how many men are beginning to turn up at them.

Invitations to tea follow the rule for any other social event involving food, except that the hour for departure is always specified.

If the invitation is to tea from 4 to 6, it means that the guest is welcome to arrive at any time convenient to her between those hours so long as she does not ring the bell just a few minutes before the party is officially over. At a very large formal tea, half an hour is considered the minimum time to stay. Forty-five minutes to one hour is more usual. At a very small tea, most guests arrive close to the earlier hour and stay for most of the specified time, though they are privileged to drop in for a shorter time if they wish.

Guests are not expected to linger more than a few minutes past the time the party's announced end, unless specifically asked to do so by the hostess.

For a very large tea, the hostess asks two

close friends to pour for her so that she may be free to welcome other guests and make introductions. This request is made at the time an invitation is given, or well in advance of the party. The guest of honor, if there is one, never is asked to take on this pleasant duty, however.

Being asked to pour is a compliment. Acceptance means a promise to be on hand a little early and to stay until the party is over. Though the pourer is sharing the duties of the hostess, she keeps her hat on, if she arrived in one. In this casual day, those who customarily go hatless are not required to rush out and buy one for a tea, though this certainly is an occasion where prettiest of afternoon dresses, immaculate gloves, and lovely hats add to the party spirit of both hostess and guests.

The experienced and thoughtful friend when accepting an invitation to pour says, "I'd love to. And is there anything I can bring?"

There well may be. Comparatively few houses today are supplied with enough tea and coffee cups for 40 or 50 guests. Borrowing a certain amount of equipment from family or close friends is general practice.

For this occasion, your prettiest china is offered, though I am always dismayed when I see irreplaceable, out-of-stock cups or plates on loan. If anything borrowed is broken or lost, the hostess is under firm obligation to replace it without delay. It is most generous, but not really kind, to give a friend the responsibility for keepsake or heirloom china that is gone forever if it is broken.

Both tea and coffee are served at a formal tea. The dining room table is spread with the prettiest lace or embroidered cloth available. At one end of the table is the tea service, on its shining bare tray. This includes a pot for tea, another for hot water, a container for any tea leaves that may remain in a cup brought back for a second pouring, a silver strainer if none is built into the pot, both granulated and lump sugar with tongs for the latter, and thin slices of

Cups, spoons, forks, or whatever else is borrowed may be brought by the guest, sent over early, or picked up by the hostess or a member of her family, whichever is the most convenient. The hostess is expected to return such possessions promptly—the next day is best—with a note of thanks if she is not going to see the lender.

lemon. Cups, saucers, and spoons are also on the table. These may be stacked attractively, if that is most convenient, though it is better to have some in reserve in the kitchen than to let the table look crowded. At the other end of the table is the coffee service. Dainty but standard-sized coffee cups are used at a tea rather than demitasses.

By tradition, curtains are drawn and candles are lighted in the room where the table is, even though it is still brightly sunny outside and curtains are not drawn in the other rooms. An exception is made on a warm afternoon when everyone is more comfortable with curtains pulled back and windows wide open to a gentle breeze, in which case candles are not lighted, of course. The heart of hospitality is making people comfortable and happy under your roof. All our rules concerning manners are based on that idea and ideal. It is simpler to follow the long-accepted standards, but it is wiser and kinder to adapt them to suit the moment when common sense dictates a change.

At the sides of the dining table between the coffee and tea services are set your daintily arranged platters of food, and dessert plates stacked with tea napkins between so that guests may make a selection of the various refreshments and carry them away from the table.

Two kinds of foods are offered at teas—savory and sweet. There may be a fairly small or a very large selection, but all should be in the daintiest of small sizes with one exception. Elaborate iced cakes needing forks are more often served at small intimate teas, though it is entirely correct to serve them at a large tea, if you wish. In this case, they are cut but left otherwise intact on a serving platter with a wide-blade server, forks, and plates handy so that guests may serve themselves.

In the savory department, the thinnest of white bread slices brushed with mayonnaise and filled with paper-thin slices of cucumber or chopped watercress are a classic at teatime.

Ribbon sandwiches are among the most effective and easy to make. Cut three thin slices of a firm-grained white bread and two slices of whole wheat. Spread a white slice with any well-seasoned filling that is not too moist. A cream cheese base is a good choice since it will not soak into the bread during the several hours of refrigeration. Now add a brown slice, more filling, then a white slice, filling, the second brown one, filling, and the third white slice. Cut off crusts. Wrap in waxed paper and chill. Slice just before serving.

Rolled sandwiches are equally effective. Remove crusts from thin slices of fresh bread. Spread with softened creamed butter and any sandwich spread that has some color for contrast. Roll and fasten with picks. Chill. Remove picks just before serving. Tuck tiny sprigs of parsley in the ends for a really festive look.

Pinwheel sandwiches are made by cutting crusts from an unsliced loaf of tender fresh bread, and cutting ¼″ slices the long way of the loaf. Spread each slice with softened butter and any well-seasoned filling mixture. The more positive the color of the filling, the more dramatic the pinwheel design will be. Roll up the full length of the slice, secure with a couple of picks, and chill. Cut in ¼″ slices just before serving.

Tiny tarts, served hot, are among the most delightful of tea dainties. These should be bite-sized, about an inch across. They may be made the day before of our Instant Mixing Pie Crust Mix or any other flaky pastry. When ready to serve, fill almost to the brim with creamed crab or any other minced sea food in a thick, hot, highly-seasoned cream sauce and pop into the oven just long enough to turn the tops golden. Especially appetizing are:

CHEESE PASTRY SHELLS

Heat oven to 425° (hot). Sift together 1 cup *sifted* GOLD MEDAL Flour and ½ tsp. salt. Cut in ¼ cup shortening, 1 cup freshly grated sharp cheese. When the mixture looks like meal, stir in 4 tsp. water. Press firmly into a smooth ball with the hands. (The mixture may seem dry at first but will work up into a ball after pressing with hands.) Roll out about ⅛″ thick. Cut into tiny rounds and press into the smallest of muffin cups or tart-shell molds. Bake *8 to 10 minutes. Makes 2½ to 3 dozen.*

The miniature Canapé Cream Puffs discussed on page 47 are delightful at teatime with either a savory or sweet filling. Try them with a mixture of chopped chicken, toasted almonds, and mayonnaise; or with minced ham, cucumber, and mayonnaise; or sea food, minced celery, and mayonnaise, all sharply seasoned. The variety is almost endless—and so are the compliments!

Tiny cream puffs are delicious with sweet fillings, also. Try whipped cream sweetened with confectioners' sugar and flavored

Afternoon Tea

Frosted Cake Fingers   Party Meringue Kisses, **p. 146**

Elegant Sandwich Loaf, **p. 126**

Appetizer Tray, see p. 52

Gay Nineties Charlotte Russe, p. 99

Fruit Crown Ring, p. 131

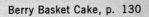
Berry Basket Cake, p. 130

Chocolate Meringue Torte, p. 98

Tossed Green Salad

Lasagne, p. 89

Tea is served with milk, never with cream. The milk is best hot, but certainly should not be ice cold since tea cools quickly at best.

with almond, or mixed with drained chopped maraschino cherries, or with finely chopped nuts.

One of the best sweet filled miniature tarts is called:

LEMON SUNSHINE TARTS

Heat oven to 425° (hot). Prepare 2 sticks Betty Crocker Instant Mixing Pie Crust Mix according to pkg. directions. Roll out dough, half at a time, to ⅛″ thick on lightly floured pastry cloth. Cut out circles 3½″ across; fit into small tart or muffin cups; flute edges; prick with fork. Bake 8 to 10 minutes, cool. Just before serving, fill each cup with 2 tbsp. Lemon Sunshine Filling. *18 to 24 tarts.*

LEMON SUNSHINE FILLING

3 eggs
2 cups sugar
grated rind of 3 lemons
   (about 5 tsp.)

½ cup lemon juice
2 tbsp. butter

Beat eggs in saucepan with rotary beater; stir in remaining ingredients. Cook over *low* heat, stirring constantly until mixture thickens. Remove from heat and cool completely.

Flowerlike petits fours with a variety of pastel-colored icings and decorations, dainty nut and date bars, shortbreads made in star or rosette shapes with a cooky press, macaroons, and icebox cookies make a tempting variety. Elaborate in appearance but simple to make in advance are:

PARTY MERINGUE KISSES

(Pictured on p. 138.)

Heat oven to 300° (slow). Blend 1 cup sugar and ⅓ cup water into 1 packet of our Betty Crocker Meringue Mix. Beat at high speed on mixer until thick and holds very stiff peaks. Drop by rounded teaspoonfuls 1″ apart on baking sheet covered with foil. Sprinkle with colored sugar, nonpareils, or finely chopped nuts. Bake *20 to 30 minutes*. Store loosely covered. *Makes about 4 dozen.*

Variants—Cherry-Nut: fold in ¼ cup chopped walnuts and 1 tbsp. chopped candied cherries. Chocolate Chip: fold in 6-oz. package (1 cup) semi-sweet chocolate pieces. Coconut: fold in 1½ cups coconut. Orange or Lemon: fold in 1 tsp. grated orange or lemon rind. Walnut: fold in ½ cup chopped walnuts.

A very rich cooky, also delicate in texture, that I find excellent for tea or many other occasions when I want an easily-handled, light, and different sweet is:

CHOCOLATE ORANGE TEA DROPS

½ cup soft butter or
  other shortening
3-oz. pkg. cream cheese
½ cup sugar
1 egg
1 tsp. grated orange rind

1 tsp. vanilla
1 cup *sifted* GOLD
  MEDAL Flour
½ tsp. salt
6-oz. pkg. semi-sweet
  chocolate pieces

Heat oven to 350° (moderate). Mix butter, cream cheese, sugar, egg, orange rind, and vanilla. Sift flour and salt together and stir in. Stir in chocolate pieces, mixing thoroughly. Drop teaspoonfuls about 1″ apart onto lightly greased baking sheet. Bake *about 15 minutes,* until cookies are delicately browned at edges. *Makes about 3 dozen cookies.*

On a cold day, guests are directed to a room where they may leave outer wraps. Women do not take off their hats at a tea, large or small. The hostess may answer the door, but she is much more free to introduce newcomers if she details a member of the family or a friend to do this for her. In summer the front door may be left standing open in welcome.

Guests make a point of finding the hostess as soon as possible after arriving. The hostess makes this easy by never getting too far away from the entrance of her living room, especially during the first hour of her tea when traffic usually is heaviest.

It is almost impossible to give a tea of any size without some help in the kitchen. Someone is needed to keep tea and coffeepots replenished, bring in extra cups and plates as they are needed, see that platters of food are well filled, and to pick up used china.

A maid—or several!—is the obvious answer, but I think the happiest solution is teen-age relatives and their friends who are too young to be guests at a grown-up tea but old enough to want to come to the party, to help, and to learn the way of hospitality by aiding in it.

A little girl is never asked to help at a tea unless her mother has been invited, of course. The youngsters are not expected to wash dishes either, since they are just as much guests as are the pourers. No great point is made of introducing them, however, as they flit back and forth, except to say casually when it is easy, "This is Janet Jones' daughter, Betty. Betty, this is Mrs. Anderson who knows your mother."

These little deputy hostesses take their tea in the kitchen—and be sure to allow twice as much for them as you do for their mothers, since the excitement of a party is sure to increase the healthy appetites of the very young.

Guests are expected to find the way to the table by themselves after greeting the hostess, except in the case of the very elderly

Milk is never served in green tea for two reasons. It overwhelms the delicate flavor and also turns the tea a dismal pallid color.

who may be seated comfortably without delay and served by the hostess or one of the group she has joined. There is good reason for letting guests serve themselves at a large tea. It is an occasion meant to bring together many friends, or those you hope will be friends. As each guest wanders back for the second cup, groups mingle more gracefully than possible if everyone remains rooted, talking all afternoon only to those who happen to be seated near.

At the beginning of a tea, the hostess introduces each newcomer to all other early arrivers, so long as the group is small and it is sensible and easy to do so. Once the party is in full swing, newcomers are introduced only to those guests near at hand, and the roof is considered introduction to everyone else under it. When a guest finds herself beside a stranger, she may chat for a moment and move along, but she usually introduces herself with something such as, "I am Mrs. Arthur Jones. I have known Alice for a long time, but we have moved to this neighborhood only recently, so I am meeting many of her friends for the first time." The other guest always responds by giving her own name, and introducing the stranger to other guests near. Then, if she wishes, she can slip away to another group. It is the greatest unkindness to the hostess, as well as most inconsiderate of the feelings of a fellow guest, to leave someone new to a gathering standing alone.

If the pourer is not serving a rush of guests, the new arrival introduces herself and stands chatting for a few minutes after accepting a cup. If the area around the table is crowded, she says no more than "Thank you," as she accepts her cup with lemon, sugar, or cream (milk for tea) added by the pourer. The guest then helps herself to sandwiches or cakes or both on a small plate, or on the edge of her saucer if she is contenting herself to only one or two, and turns back toward the living room where she joins any group she chooses. If she is a stranger, the hostess takes particular pains to introduce her to a group, or may say to another friend, "Mary, I know Mrs. Jones and Mrs. Burkhardt will enjoy comparing notes on flower shows. Will you see that they meet?" Every guest makes a point of having a few words with the guest of honor, introducing herself, if that is the simple, easy thing to do, or reminding the hostess when she has a free minute, "I must leave soon, and I do so want to meet your reason for this good party." Conversation with a guest of honor may be of the briefest, but a guest should not leave without exchanging a few words with her.

When it is time to leave, the guest puts down her cup and plate on a sideboard or any convenient surface, though preferably not a prominent one in the living room, especially if the party is still young. She has already thanked the pourer when she was served. She need not make a point of saying good-bye to her unless she has some special reason for doing so. It is enough to find the hostess, thank her for a pleasant time, and go. Unless the hostess is swamped with a rush of guests arriving and leaving at the same time, she goes to the door with the one who is departing. If she has to choose between being in two places at once, common sense dictates concentrating on introductions, rather than farewells that take her to the door, and she settles for a gracious good-bye in her living room.

A tea table, large or small, is spread with a cloth, but the trays under tea and coffee services always are used without a covering.

The routine for a small tea is quite different from that of the large one. The hostess most often telephones an invitation, but under any circumstances makes it clear that the party is a small one since the guest at a small tea is expected to arrive at, or soon after the hour at which the party starts and to stay fairly well through the specified time. If she must be quite late, or must leave quite early, it is considerate to give an explanation when accepting. One might say, "I'd love to come, but I must take the Cub Scouts swimming. May I join you after five instead of four?" or "I'll be there on the dot so I can have as much time as possible with you. I have to pick up the children from dancing class right after five."

The hostess serving an intimate group has her tea service on a tray ready to be carried in to a coffee table, or wheeled in on the invaluable teacart, soon after her guests arrive. On the tray should be the teapot, an extra pot of boiling water for those who like a pale brew, strainer, tongs, milk, lemon in thin slices rather than wedges. Plates and tea napkins, cups and saucers, platters of sandwiches, cookies, and cakes are also at hand. If there is not room on the coffee table, use a small tea table covered with a cloth.

The hostess asks each guest her wishes, and then adds sugar, milk, or lemon. She hands cups to those within reach. Other guests come over to the tea table for their cups. If it is difficult or awkward for any guest to rise for her cup, the hostess anticipates such an ef-

Tea bags are not used at a tea party. They have their useful place at family meals when one or two members only want a quick hot drink, but they are not used at parties with any pretention to formality.

The hostess serves one cup at a time, since the rule is that tea is passed directly from the hand of the pourer to the guest. This convention came about because tea cools quickly.

fort by taking it to her unless some observant friend rises to help. Here again, small collapsible tables, if you have them, are invaluable for china and ash trays. Otherwise, try to seat guests near other surfaces that may substitute for tables.

Any of the small sandwiches, cakes, tarts, cream puffs, and cookies suitable for a large tea are good choices for a small one, though it is not customary to offer such a wide variety. A small plate of savory sandwiches, buttered slices of a rich nut loaf, and small rich cookies are enough. Many people concentrate on just one beautiful cake. A lovely one is:

PINK AZALEA CAKE

Make cake as directed on our Betty Crocker White Cake Mix package. Tint 1/3 of the batter a delicate pink with food coloring. Bake in three 8″ layer pans, *about* 18 minutes. Make a pink icing by tinting a package of our Betty Crocker Fluffy White Frosting Mix with 3 or 4 drops of red food coloring. Into ⅓ of the icing fold ⅓ cup well-drained cut-up strawberries. Spread this between the layers. Frost top and sides of the cake with the remaining icing.

Small teas are the time for rare or special blends of tea. The variety is almost endless. One of my friends has a collection of over 30, ranging from strong black so-called Breakfast teas through amber-colored Oolongs, some scented with jasmine or other flower petals, to the greenish-gold of the Green teas. She keeps them in air-tight tins so they preserve their flavor indefinitely. She has never

For flavored sugars, combine 2 tbsp. of chopped fresh mint, or grated orange or lemon rind, with one lb. of superfine sugar in a tightly closed jar for a week. Sift before using in tea.

served the same tea to me twice. All are delicious, and their novelty makes them seem doubly so. Very often she also has a choice of plain and flavored sugars for an added adventure in taste. Flavored sugars are good in either hot or iced tea, and are easy to make.

Benefit teas follow the rules for the entirely social affairs except that the invitation always specifically mentions the purpose for which donations are requested, such as "A silver tea for benefit of the Women's Guild." This means that guests are expected to leave some silver coins in a tray, usually placed near the door, on departure. Or "A white elephant tea for benefit of the Missionary Society's Swap Shop," means that each guest is expected to bring some of those unwanted or duplicate gifts all of us accumulate.

For these occasions the more guests, the more successful the collection will be. Even so, the experienced guest does not turn up with several uninvited friends, no matter how generously they will contribute. Just as she would for any other social event, she telephones the hostess for permission to bring someone with her.

Fruit punches often are substituted for coffee and tea at large afternoon receptions, and they are especially welcome in hot weather. The ideal service for them is a big glass or crystal punch bowl and matching punch cups. Pressed glass punch sets are surprisingly inexpensive, and worth putting on your Christmas list of hoped-for gifts. Here are several party punches I have enjoyed at teas, and they are equally good before a lunch or dinner.

CIDER PUNCH

2 cups orange juice

1 cup lemon juice

4 cups apple cider

1 cup *sifted* confectioners' sugar

Combine juices with sugar and stir well. Pour over ice cubes. *12 servings.*

SPICED FRUIT PUNCH

2½ cups orange juice

1 cup canned pineapple juice

2 cups cold water

½ cup confectioners' sugar

2 tbsp. grated lemon rind

1 tbsp. honey

6 whole cloves

½ tsp. nutmeg

½ tsp. cinnamon

6 cups ginger ale

Combine all ingredients except ginger ale. Let stand for 3 hours. Strain. Add ginger ale and crushed ice. *Makes about 15 cups.*

GRAPE JUICE CRUSH

2 cups grape juice

1 cup orange juice

¼ cup lemon juice

½ cup sugar

2 cups ice water

1 qt. chilled ginger ale

Mix all ingredients except ginger ale. Add it just before serving in glasses partly filled with cracked ice. *12 servings.*

PARTY PUNCH

4 qt. water

3 cups sugar

two 6-oz. cans lemon juice

1 qt. apple juice

2 qt. cranberry juice

1 pt. orange juice

1 pt. strong black tea

Bring water and sugar to boiling. Combine with remaining ingredients and chill before serving. *Makes 2 gal. or 40 servings.*

Brunch

BRUNCH MOST frequently is a week end event since that is a time when many people sleep late and combine breakfast and lunch in one substantial meal.

Brunch is served anywhere from 10 to noon. It is rather more akin to an elaborate breakfast than to lunch, though a certain number of dishes suitable for lunch may be offered, and porridge or other cereals usually are not served.

Service always is easy-going and informal, whether you have a maid or not. The table is covered with a fairly simple cloth of white or colored linen, or a gaily printed or cross-stitched one in preference to a handsomely embroidered or lacy one. Placemats are an equally good choice.

Food may be on the table, family style, with the host in charge of the main dishes and the hostess pouring coffee and passing cups along from guest to guest. For a large group and a fairly large variety of dishes, the so-called "English Breakfast Service" is by far the most convenient. This means that main course

CREAMED HARD-COOKED EGGS on canned Chinese noodles that have been crisped in the oven are a tempting combination of velvety sauce and crunchy base.

dishes are on a sideboard in covered dishes kept warm over hot plates or chafing dish flames. Each guest helps himself before taking a place at the table.

In either case, the first course is on the table, and the hostess usually serves coffee from her place. Many refills are to be expected as this meal takes its leisurely course, and it is more peaceful for everyone if guests do not pop up and down each time a cup is empty.

If an invitation to brunch mentions a specific hour, a small gathering is implied and the good guest arrives on the dot. Often invitations to brunch give the guest more latitude, such as "Come to brunch after eleven." This implies that quite a sizeable number are expected, and that the guest is privileged to arrive exactly at that hour, or drift in a little later. Half an hour is about the limit of leeway a thoughtful guest will take, however.

The single most important rule for brunch is "Serve promptly." Knowing that a generous spread is waiting, the late risers will content themselves with coffee and fruit and little else. They will arrive ravenous, and the party spirit dims rapidly if there is any delay. This is no time to stand on ceremony and wait until all guests arrive. Ten minutes past the announced hour is enough to wait for a late-comer. After the meal has started, the host answers the door and brings the dilatory guests to the table. They go to the hostess, who does not rise from her place. She gives them cordial greeting and directs them to their places where a first course is waiting.

Orange, pineapple, tomato, or other juices are the safest of all starters at brunch. These should be on the table in glasses set at the water glass location directly above the knife. Water is not usually served at brunch. Grapefruit, melon, berries, or sliced peaches are delightful first courses but I never choose them except for the smallest of groups since clearing their dishes away means some delay in getting down to the important business of solid hot food.

Variety is part of the charm of brunch, but any menu that calls for short-order cooking puts too many demands on the hostess. Brunch is no time to fry, poach, or boil eggs to suit each individual, especially when there are so many tempting ways to serve eggs without flurry—scrambled, baked on a base of ground ham or chicken, poached and served on a bed of puréed spinach under a rich cream sauce, or on a steaming-hot corned beef hash.

One of the best egg dishes I know is akin to Eggs Benedict. It looks, tastes, and is elaborate, and is well worth the advance preparation needed for easy serving.

SMOKED TURKEY AND EGGS SUPREME

Top a warm toasted English muffin with a slice of smoked turkey and then a heap of soft scrambled eggs. Cover with about 3 tbsp. warm Hollandaise sauce and a sprinkling of chopped chives.

For dishes that can be kept hot over low heat until everyone has had a second helping, good choices are chipped beef, salmon, cubed ham or chicken in a cream sauce, and, of course, broiled bacon, ham, sausages, or hot kippers.

Tomatoes are exceptionally good with egg dishes. I like them cut in half crosswise or in very thick slices, brushed with butter, sprinkled lightly with any salad herb and a dash of nutmeg, and broiled rather briefly so that they maintain their shape.

Big mushroom caps, seasoned with salt and pepper and broiled, are another most appetizing companion to eggs.

With sausage, I like tart apple rings, broiled in butter or bacon grease, under a glaze of honey, brown sugar, maple syrup, or jelly.

The best centerpiece for the brunch table is a Lazy Susan. On it can be placed a choice of marmalade, jam and jelly, as well as salt, pepper, sugar, cream, butter, syrups, or anything else needed in easy reach of each guest.

When I am serving brunch to six or fewer, I sometimes put a toaster on the table and appoint one guest "toast master" for all of us. For a larger group, I choose muffins, rolls, hot biscuits, Sally Lunn, corn bread, or some other dainty hot bread. They seem just a little more thoughtful and partylike than toast, popular as it is, and they are somewhat easier to keep in good supply, since reserves can wait in the warming oven for a reasonable time.

Waffles are a universal favorite. For a small group these are a happy choice made at the table. They are also good made in advance and brought back to crisp perfection in the oven just before serving a larger number. To keep waffles warm: place between folds of warm towel in warm oven. Or place waffles separately on rack in very low oven with door ajar. (Don't stack them!)

A rich coffee cake is a standard item at brunch. An exceptionally pretty and easy one to make is:

BUTTER-BALL COFFEE CAKE

2 cans Betty Crocker
   Bisquick Refrigerated
   Biscuits
¼ cup butter, melted

¾ cup sugar
1 tbsp. cinnamon
¼ cup chopped nuts

Heat oven to 375° (quick moderate). Grease a 9″ round layer pan. Separate biscuits and dip in melted butter, then coat each entirely with a mixture of the sugar and cinnamon. Place 15 biscuits around the outer part of the pan, overlapping to make a circle. Overlap remaining 5 biscuits to fill center. Pour remaining butter over. Sprinkle with chopped nuts. Bake *25 to 30 minutes.* Allow to stand 5 minutes before serving. The rich, buttery biscuits break apart easily.

Unless the invitation to brunch includes some plan for the afternoon, such as sharing a particular television show, or playing some game such as croquet or tennis, the party is over about an hour after the last cup of coffee is served, and guests are expected to leave the hostess to a well-deserved nap.

Barbecues

THE WELL-PLANNED barbecue is one of the most delightful of meals. It is pleasant to be out of doors in the warm summer dusk with the companionship of the hostess who has to take no time out in the kitchen. The savory aroma of meat grilling over charcoal, as the host deftly brushes the sizzling feast with basting sauce, is an appetizer in itself.

One of the charms of meals cooked *al fresco* is the informality of spirit and service, though I see no excuse for good indoor manners to be forgotten.

The lawn surrounding the barbecue grill is an outdoor living room. Flower beds are not ash trays, and neither is the fire. City dwellers do not always understand that small bones, tossed off into a concealing bed of ivy, may attract a convention of ants, or send a little dog to the veterinary for a painful and expensive session.

"Don't ever ask that guy again!" I heard a host say to his wife about a too-busy guest who was stirring the fire, turning steaks, and adding ingredients to the sauce without being asked.

CHARCOAL GRILLED BARBECUED CHICKEN

Allow time for gray ash to cover charcoal briquets, about 45 minutes. Spread coals ½″ apart with poker or long stick. Tap off outer ashes just before, and occasionally during barbecuing. Brush grill with fat to keep meat from sticking. Brush chicken broiler pieces with Barbecue Sauce (recipe below) or marinate in sauce while getting the fire ready. Drain off excess sauce. Set chicken on grill 6 to 8″ from coals. If distance has to be less, watch carefully to avoid charring. Keep turning chicken every 5 minutes, basting with sauce, 30 to 60 minutes, depending on size.

Barbecue Sauce

1 cup tomato purée
  or catsup
½ cup water
⅓ cup lemon juice
¼ cup soft butter
1 medium onion,
  finely chopped

1 tbsp. paprika
1 tbsp. Worcestershire
  sauce
1 tsp. sugar
1 tsp. salt
½ tsp. pepper

Mix all ingredients and bring just to boil. If sauce thickens on standing, dilute with water to good spreading consistency. Keep sauce hot for basting. *Enough for two broilers.*

BASTING SAUCE FOR FISH

1 chicken bouillon cube
½ cup boiling water
1 cup butter, melted
2 tbsp. lemon juice
1 tsp. soy sauce

½ tsp. Worcestershire
  sauce
1 tsp. paprika
¼ tsp. salt

Dissolve chicken bouillon cube in boiling water. Add rest of ingredients. Pour over fish and baste while grilling.

Try serving these Sparerib Bites as an appetizer while the main course is barbecuing.

SWEET-SOUR SPARERIB BITES

3 lb. small, lean spareribs (have the butcher cut the
    ribs in half crosswise, so each is about 2″ long)
½ lemon
½ cup finely chopped onion (1 medium)

Heat oven to 450° (hot). Separate ribs by cutting between each with kitchen shears. Place pieces of rib in shallow baking pan. Do not cover. Do not add water. Sprinkle lightly with salt and pepper. Cut lemon into very thin slices, then in quarters. Sprinkle lemon and onion over meat. Roast *45 minutes,* to brown. Pour Sweet-Sour Sauce (recipe below) over ribs. *Reduce heat to 350° (moderate). Continue roasting 1 hour.* Baste with sauce about every 15 minutes. If sauce gets too thick, add a little hot water. *12 to 16 servings.*

Sweet-Sour Sauce

½ tsp. chili powder
½ tsp. salt
dash of pepper
1½ tsp. celery seeds
2 tbsp. brown sugar
few drops Tabasco sauce,
    if desired

2 tbsp. vinegar
2 tbsp. Worcestershire
    sauce
½ cup catsup
½ cup water

Mix all ingredients and bring to a boil.

Big pink shrimp are superb grilled with mushrooms and ham in a sharp sauce, and one of the prettiest of skewered foods. Or try grilling Rock Lobster tails.

CHARCOAL GRILLED
ROCK LOBSTER TAILS

Plunge lobster tails into boiling salted water. Bring back to boil and simmer 10 minutes per lb. Drain. When briquets are covered with gray ash and very hot, place lobster tails on grill, shell-side-down, 3 or 4″ above briquets. Cook 15 to 20 minutes. Brush generously with melted butter or margarine, turn, and cook 3 to 5 minutes longer. Season with coarse, freshly ground black pepper and salt to taste. Serve with melted butter or margarine and lemon wedges.

Success Tip: Do not overcook lobster tails as they tend to become tough when overdone.

Shish-kabobs are a classic at the outdoor grill, and one of the wisest choices since meat and vegetables are produced in one savory serving. Tender beef, cut in 1″ or slightly larger cubes, will go decidedly farther skewered with mushrooms, onion slices, and green peppers than as individual steaks.

Veal is superb cooked on skewers with bits of bacon, though caution should be taken not to overcook since veal becomes dry rapidly. Give it no more time than you would allow for medium-well-done steak, and it will stay juicy, succulent, and magnificently tender.

Here is a recipe that never fails to please:

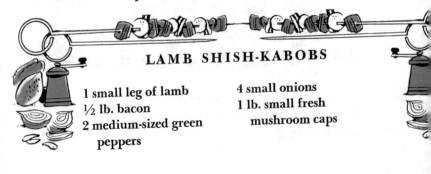

LAMB SHISH-KABOBS

1 small leg of lamb
½ lb. bacon
2 medium-sized green peppers

4 small onions
1 lb. small fresh mushroom caps

Cut meat in 1" cubes, removing all fat and gristle. Marinate in Sauce (recipe below) several hours or overnight, turning occasionally so that all pieces are well soaked. Just before making kabobs, partially pan broil bacon and cut in 1" pieces. Cut green peppers in 1" pieces and pour boiling water over them. Drain. Slice onions very thin. Alternate meats and vegetables on a long thin skewer allowing space between each. Broil 5" from source of heat about 15 to 20 minutes, turning frequently. *20 to 25 kabobs.*

Marinade Sauce

½ cup olive oil	3 tsp. salt
¼ cup white wine vinegar	1 tsp. oregano
2 tbsp. sherry flavoring	¼ tsp. dry basil
juice and rind of 1 lemon	¼ tsp. freshly ground pepper
	4 cloves garlic, crushed

Combine all ingredients and mix with rotary beater until well blended.

Though the host usually seems to be doing all of the work at a barbecue, the success of this meal depends in large part on advance planning and preparation so that there is no racing back and forth to the house for supplies. Everything he needs in the way of seasonings, tools, serving dishes, and silver should be at hand near the fire before guests arrive.

Salad and dressing should be waiting, in the refrigerator, to be tossed, and vegetables should be ready for the fire.

Some of my friends find it simpler to cook vegetables in the kitchen. This is most practical if the outdoor grill is extremely small, but it seems to me much more fun to barbecue vegetables as well as meat, if the grill can accommodate them.

There are two schools of passionately-held thought about potatoes roasted in the open. There are those who claim that either sweet or Irish potatoes left on coals until the outsides are charred are the very soul of outdoor cookery. Others retort that a burned potato is a mistake anywhere. Take your choice. Mealy, soft-skinned potatoes are easily produced on a grill by wrapping them securely in foil and letting them steam at the edge of the coals, turning frequently.

Onions may be wrapped in foil with a little butter for a delicate taste, but the most delicious grilled onions I ever ate were sizzled and blackened right on top of the coals. For this method order the really enormous Bermuda onions, the bigger the better, since several of their outside layers will be lost. Put them on the grill or around the edges of the coals. When they are tender to the heart, shuck off the black, charred outside layers with hands protected by asbestos gloves. The inside will be a golden yellow, sweet and with no flavor of charring but with a roasted taste quite different from foil-wrapped ones.

Corn comes from foil tender and steaming, but again I like it best done by the classic corn-roast method.

CHARCOAL GRILLED CORN

Allow time for gray ash to cover charcoal briquets, about 45 minutes. Discard outer husks. Strip inner husks to end of cob; do not tear off. Pull out silk. Soak in ice water 20 minutes. Drain corn on towel; leave husks wet. Spread corn generously with butter. Rewrap in husks; then in double thickness of heavy duty aluminum foil. Cook on ash gray coals 10 to 15 minutes, turning once.

Success Tip: Salt toughens corn so season *after* cooking.

Acorn squash is another vegetable that may be tossed whole into the coals. The outside will char, but that does not matter. Split the squash when done, scoop out seeds, and serve with 1 tbsp. of the following sauce in each steaming half.

SAUCE FOR BAKED SQUASH
(Pictured on p. 39.)

½ cup butter, melted	1 clove garlic, crushed
½ cup honey	1 tsp. salt
3 tbsp. sweet chow chow	⅛ tsp. pepper
1 tbsp. chili powder	⅛ tsp. nutmeg

Mix all ingredients; serve warm or cold. Spoon a little sauce into hollows of baked acorn or hubbard squash. *Makes about 1 cup.*

Garlic bread, wrapped in foil, heats just as well at the edge of a grill as it does in the oven. Remove the foil when bread is thoroughly hot, and toast briefly.

SPIEDINI
(pronounced spee-a-dee-nee)

Cut a loaf of French Bread in ¾″ thick slices but do not cut slices completely through. Place a thin slice of Mozzarella cheese between each bread slice. Tuck tiny bits of anchovy fillet here and there among the cheese and bread slices. With loaf on baking sheet, pour ½ cup melted butter over loaf. Heat in 350° oven until cheese melts, 10 to 15 minutes. Sprinkle with minced parsley and serve immediately.

ANCHOVY BUTTER is easy to make and wonderful with steaks, chops, and fish. Cream ¼ lb. butter with 1 tsp. anchovy paste.

FROZEN VEGETABLES may be cooked on a grill by taking them from the package, dotting with butter, sprinkling with salt, and wrapping while still frozen in heavy foil. Turn once during cooking, which takes 30 to 35 minutes.

Cake, pie, cookies, and ice cream, or watermelon are good barbecue desserts. Here is one your guests will surely enjoy.

DATE BARS WITH OLD-FASHIONED LEMON SAUCE

Follow directions on Betty Crocker Date Bar Mix package. Serve warm cut in squares. Top with whipped cream. Pour Old-fashioned Lemon Sauce over.

Old-fashioned Lemon Sauce

½ cup butter
1 cup sugar
¼ cup water
1 egg, well beaten

3 tbsp. lemon juice
  (1 lemon)
grated rind of 1 lemon

Mix all ingredients in saucepan. Cook over medium heat, stirring constantly, just until mixture comes to a boil. *Makes 1⅓ cups sauce.*

Toss branches of bay or laurel into your fire at the end of cooking time for a tempting perfume and extra flavor, or, if you have an overgrown herb bed, a handful of thyme or marjoram leaves.

House Parties

"Just do as you would be done by—and have a happy time," is standard instruction to youngsters venturing off to visit relatives overnight for the first time.

At no time is the Golden Rule a better guide for both hostess and guest than at a house party, starting with invitation and acceptance.

The guest cannot help being uncertain and ill-at-ease unless invitations are explicit about both the time of arrival and of departure, and any special plans that might call for bathing suit, dinner dress, hiking shoes, or other equipment. A good form is:

"We want you for the whole week end. There is a good fast train arriving here at 6 on Friday. I will meet you. We are going to take you to the club for dancing Saturday night, and Sunday we'll have dinner on the shore, so do plan to stay over and go in with Joe on the 8:30 Monday morning."

Those few words tell the guest what to plan and pack. The acceptance must be equally explicit. If at all possible, it is best to arrive at the time suggested by the hostess who has chosen it for her convenience as well as yours. If that is awkward, it is reasonable to say, "I can't get away from the office quite so early? Is the next train all right?" or "I find I can get a lift with some friends. Will it be convenient if they drop me as early as 5:30?" Under any circumstances, the time should be fairly near that suggested by the hostess. If it is not convenient for you to stay for the whole week end, tell your hostess when you must be at home, and let her suggest the best time for departure.

On arrival, the guest is shown the quarters he will occupy, whether a couch in the living room or room with its own bath, and allowed a few minutes to unpack and freshen up. This is a chance to explain bathroom arrangements, location of towels and soap, and to find out when a guest prefers a shower.

The hostess makes the first move to retire at the end of the evening. She usually goes with a guest to see that windows are open, blinds drawn, and everything needed for the night is at hand. This includes something to read, a glass of water, and always the offer of something to eat. Many people like a snack just before retiring and spend a restless night without it. A small plate of fruit and cookies on a bedside table is thoughtful and usually most welcome. The hostess may turn down the bed, or leave that for the guest to do. In either case, the spread is removed and neatly folded, never tossed aside or left on the bed.

"We have breakfast at nine," is an indication that the hostess will be pleased if everyone turns up for that meal on time. If she adds, "But you sleep as late as you like," the guest understands that it is entirely convenient to put in an appearance any time before noon. The thoughtful hostess also makes provision for those who wake with the earliest birds. She says something such as, "I'll be up at eight, but if you want coffee before that, slip down and start it. Everything is ready on the range, and the newspaper will be on the porch." In this case, it is entirely proper to seek coffee in a pretty negligee or robe, though, if it develops that host and hostess dress before breakfast, follow their lead before joining them at the table.

When visiting a house without help, the good guest is alert to do a fair share about preparation of meals and washing of dishes. And the good hostess accepts a certain amount of help since it is embarrassing to most guests to sit idly by while she is hard at work.

On the other hand, if a hostess says, "Now I want you to rest. Dinner is all planned. It won't take me any time to start it. Why don't you get some sun in the garden?" the understanding guest takes this as a signal that the hostess needs a few minutes to herself, and retires for a nap or a quiet time with a book.

So far as possible, the guest falls in with any plans suggested. You may take a dim view of the local chamber-music sextet, but if tickets have been reserved for their concert, go along as if you would like nothing better. You might be pleasantly surprised. In any case, you can't escape and it is better to give in gracefully. Of course, if a day of hiking is planned and you have a bad ankle, it is absurd not to mention that you'll need to be carried home.

House-party breakfasts are one of the pleasantest of meals, to me. This is the time when the inner circle sits around enjoying the special intimacy of food at the beginning of the day.

When there are several guests, buffet service of certain parts of breakfast is both easiest and most tempting. It is not always easy to determine individual preferences in advance, so I set forth a variety of foods that are not perishable. It is attractive and little trouble to set a buffet or Lazy Susan with a choice of several dry cereals, a bowl of berries or sliced fruit, cream (or soft ice cream for a festive touch), white, brown, and vanilla-flavored sugars, and let each guest choose. In winter hot cooked rolled oats is an excellent choice. Nearly everyone had breakfast porridge as a child, but some have forgotten how delicious it is with fruits, dates, brown sugar, honey, and cream dusted with nutmeg or cinnamon. Try it, and be astonished at the compliments you will get from your most sophisticated friends.

In a house I love to visit, we have breakfast in a big kitchen that has plenty of room for a table at which family and guests can sit comfortably. This is a perfect arrangement for the serving of pancakes. Our hostess keeps them coming from a range-top griddle, sipping coffee as she keeps our plates heaped with cakes, crisp bacon or sausage, maple syrup, or honey whipped with butter.

House-party breakfasts are the ideal time for waffles or popovers, cloud-light right out of the oven, and, for the last course, the whole big family of coffee cakes and Danish pastries.

The house guest is expected to keep a bedroom in order in any but an establishment with a large staff. This means no more than making the bed, emptying ash trays, and returning to the kitchen any used glasses or plates.

On leaving, the guest usually turns covers back, though, if there is time, it is thoughtful to ask the hostess for fresh linen and offer to remake the bed for her.

Of course, you thank your hostess on departure, but no matter how enthusiastic you are in words, a formal "bread and butter" note is required after any overnight visit, and some small gift is usual. This may be a present you take with you, or something you send within the following week.

House presents need not be expensive, but imagination and awareness of the household's needs is most important.

Children often are pushed somewhat in the background during a week end devoted to adult guests. Those who arrive with a present for the youngsters make a special hit with them, as well as their parents. This can be a book, candy, or a game, but time and again I have seen such minor toys as balloons, skipping ropes, or yo-yos for the whole gang make the biggest success. Remember that children love best the toys that give them something to do—and so do grown-ups.

Among the most effective gifts for a hostess are unusual delicacies. These can be a selection of tinned appetizer snacks, an unusual cheese, a rare honey, but best of all, I think, is some specialty from a friend's own kitchen—a jar of marmalade, jam, jelly, pickles, a homemade fruitcake, or a prettily packed tin or box of cookies.

Remember then, that hospitality is as we said earlier "being disposed to entertain with generous kindness." With planning you can be ready for entertaining in practical detail as well as in spirit; and don't forget to "entertain" yourself as well as others.

Best wishes for many relaxed and happy hours with your guests.

variety is the spice of life!

Almond oven-fried chicken, 65
Almond soup, cream of, 124
Almonds, sautéed, 51
Anadama batter bread, 97
Anchovy butter, 165
Angel food cake, baked
    Alaska, 71
Appetizers, *see also* Canapés
  almonds, sautéed, 51
  cheese Kix, 51
  chili dip, 48
  cider, mulled, 52
  guacamole, 48
  minced clam-cheese dip, 49
  shrimp remoulade, 49
  sparerib bites, sweet-sour, 161
  suggestions for, 45-52
  tomato juice, 52
Apricot mousse supreme, 70
Arctic cooler, 74
Artichokes, serving suggestions,
    64
Avocado
  mousse, 60
  serving suggestions, 64

Baked Alaska angel food cake,
    71
Baked bean and sausage
    casserole, 87
Barbecued chicken,
    charcoal grilled, 160
Basting sauce for fish, 160
Bean and sausage casserole,
    baked, 87
Beans
  green, serving suggestions,
    68, 93
  Lima, serving suggestions, 68
Berry basket cake, 130

Beverages, *see also* Cider ;
    Coffee ; Punch ; Tea
  buffet dinner, 80
  midnight supper, 111
  Smorgasbord, 91
Bread
  anadama batter, 97
  for lunches, 128, 129
  for Smorgasbord, 91
  garlic, heated outdoors, 165
  herb batter, 129
  herb loaf, 96
  sandwich loaf, 126
  spiedini, 165
Broccoli, Italian, 69
Brownie peppermint pie, 115
Butter, anchovy, 165
Butter-ball coffee cake, 158

Café Mexicain, 77
Cake
  baked Alaska angel food, 71
  berry basket, 130
  chocolate chiffon, "lovelight,"
    118, icing for, 119
  chocolate cream "lovelight,"
    119
  fruitcake, remembrance, 112
  lemon coconut, 114
  pink azalea, 151
Cake filling, Maggie's
    butter-nut, 107
Canadian cheese soup, 124
Canapé cream puffs, 47
  deviled cheese filling for, 47
  serving suggestions, 136
Canapés, *see also* Appetizers
  Chinese water chestnut, 50
  cocktail surprises, 51
  green leaf, 46

  mushroom, 47
  serving suggestions, 45
  shrimp remoulade, 49
  suggestions for, 45-47, 50
Carrots, serving
    suggestions, 68
Cauliflower, serving
    suggestions, 69
Celery Louisianne, 62
Celery root and grape salad, 61
Charcoal grilled barbecued
    chicken, 160
Charcoal grilled corn, 164
Charcoal grilled rock lobster
    tails, 162
Cheese
  accompaniments for, 111
  canapés, green leaf, 46
  cream, *see* Cream cheese
  deviled, filling for canapé
    cream puffs, 47
  for midnight supper, 111
  for Smorgasbord, 91
  Kix, 51
  pastry shells, 136
  serving suggestions, 111
  snacks, 63
  soup, Canadian, 124
  spiedini, 165
Cherry glaze, for ham. 86
Chicken
  almond oven-fried, 65
  barbecued, charcoal grilled,
    160
  oven-baked, with orange
    sauce, 66-67
  Parisian, 66
  Parmesan oven-fried, 65
  pie, Irene's, topped with
    savory pastry, 127

Chili
  dip, 48
  spicy, 118
Chinese veal, 67
Chinese water chestnut
  canapés, 50
Chocolate
  chiffon cake, "lovelight," 118
    icing for, 119
  cream cake, "lovelight," 119
  meringue torte, 98
  orange tea drops, 146
  puffs, French silk, 108
Cider
  mulled, 52
  punch, 153
  serving suggestions, 52
Clam-cheese dip, minced, 49
Cocktail surprises, 51
Coconut cake, lemon, 114
Coffee
  Arctic cooler, 74
  Café Mexicain, 77
  egg, 74
  serving suggestions, 73-77,
    100, 134, 154, 155
  sesame honey demitasse, 76
Coffee cake, butter-ball, 158
Colonial innkeeper's pie, 72
Cookies
  chocolate orange tea drops,
    146
  party meringue kisses, 146
  Wheaties nougat bars, 115
Corn, charcoal grilled, 164
Cranberry juice, 52
Cream cheese
  canapés, 46
  minced clam-cheese dip, 49
Cream of almond soup, 124
Cream puffs
  canapé, 47
  chocolate, French silk, 108
  deviled cheese filling for, 47
  serving suggestions, 136

Cucumber and tomato soup,
  chilled, 63

Date bars with old-fashioned
  lemon sauce, 166
Dessert, suggestions for
  barbecue, 166
  buffet meals, 81, 98-99
  lunch, 129-131
  midnight supper, 114-115
  pot luck dinner, 103
  stag parties, 118-119
Desserts, *see also* Cake;
  Cookies; Pie
  apricot mousse supreme, 70
  baked Alaska angel food
    cake, 71
  berry basket cake, 130
  Charlotte russe, gay nineties,
    99
  chocolate meringue torte, 98
  colonial innkeeper's pie, 72
  date bars with old-fashioned
    lemon sauce, 166
  French silk chocolate puffs,
    108
  fruit crown ring, 131
  ice cream polka dot, 98-99
Deviled cheese filling for
  canapé cream puffs, 47

Egg coffee, 74
Eggs
  creamed hard-cooked,
    on Chinese noodles, 155
  serving suggestions for
    brunch, 156-157
  supreme, and smoked turkey,
    156
Elegant sandwich loaf, 126
Emergency rations, list of,
  105-106

Filling, Maggie's
  butter-nut cake, 107

Fish, *see also* Sea food
  basting sauce for, 160
Flavored sugars, 152
French silk chocolate puffs, 108
Fruit crown ring, 131
Fruit juice, as appetizer, 52
Fruit punch, spiced, 153
Fruitcake, remembrance, 112

Garlic bread
  heating outdoors, 165
  substitute for, 96
Gay nineties Charlotte russe, 99
Glaze, cherry, for ham, 86
Gold and white salad, 94-95
Gourmet potato salad, 117
Grape and celery root salad, 61
Grape juice crush, 153
Green beans in sour cream, 93
Green leaf canapés, 46
Guacamole (dip), 48

Ham
  and turkey Tetrazzini, 113
  serving suggestions
    (buffet style), 82-83, 85
  Washington cherry glaze for,
    86
Hearts of palm salad, 64
Herb batter bread, 129
Herb loaf, 96

Ice cream
  baked Alaska angel food
    cake, 71
  polka dot dessert, 98-99
Icing, white mountain, 119
Italian broccoli, 69

Kix, cheese, 51

Lamb
  leg of, stuffed, 86
  shish-kabobs, 162-163

Lasagne, 89
Lemon coconut cake, 114
Lemon sunshine tarts, 145
  filling for, 145
Lima beans,
  serving suggestions, 68
Lobster tails, charcoal grilled,
  rock, 162
"Lovelight" chocolate chiffon
  cake, 118
"Lovelight" chocolate cream
  cake, 119

Marshmallow-date sweet
  potatoes, 93
Menus
  dinner made from emergency
    rations, 105
  small dinner party, 59
Meringue kisses, party, 146
Meringue torte, chocolate, 98
Minced clam-cheese dip, 49
Mousse
  apricot, supreme, 70
  avocado, 60
Mulled cider, 52
Mushroom canapés, 47

Nougat bars, Wheaties, 115

Olive creamed potatoes, 94
Onions, grilled, 164
Orange tea drops, chocolate,
  146
Oven-baked chicken with
  orange sauce, 66-67

Parmesan oven-fried chicken,
  65
Party meringue kisses, 146
Party punch, 153
Pastry, *see also* Pie
  shells, cheese, 136
  tarts, lemon sunshine, 145

Peach fruit mold, spiced, 95
Peaches, canned, serving
  suggestions, 93
Peppermint pie, brownie, 115
Pie
  brownie peppermint, 115
  chicken, Irene's, topped with
    savory pastry, 127
  colonial innkeeper's, 72
Pink azalea cake, 151
Pork
  chops, stuffed, with
    pineapple-orange dressing,
    68
  sweet-sour sparerib bites, 161
Potato salad, gourmet, 117
Potatoes
  olive creamed, 94
  sweet, marshmallow-date, 93
Punch, 153
  cider, 153
  grape juice crush, 153
  party, 153
  spiced fruit, 153

Rations, emergency, list of,
  105-106

Salad
  avocado mousse, 60
  celery root and grape, 61
  celery Louisianne, 62
  gold and white, 94-95
  hearts of palm, 64
  molded fruit, 95
  potato, gourmet, 117
Sandwich loaf, elegant, 126
Sandwiches
  pinwheel, suggestions for, 136
  ribbon, suggestions for, 135
  rolled, suggestions for, 135
  spiedini, 165
Sauce
  basting, for fish, 160
  for baked squash, 165

Sausage and baked bean
  casserole, 87
Sea food, *see also* Fish
  lobster tails, charcoal grilled,
    rock, 162
Shrimp de jonghe, 125
Sesame honey demitasse, 76
Shish-kabobs, lamb, 162-163
Shrimp
  de Jonghe, 125
  grilled, with mushrooms and
    ham, 161
  remoulade, 49
Smorgasbord, 90-91
Soup
  accompaniments for, 63
  Canadian cheese, 124
  chilled tomato and
    cucumber, 63
  cold, 61-62
  cream of almond, 124
  vichyssoise, 62
Sparerib bites, sweet-sour, 161
Spiced fruit punch, 153
Spiced peach fruit mold, 95
Spicy chili, 118
Spiedini, 165
Squash
  acorn, cooked outdoors, 164
  baked, sauce for, 165
  continental, 92
Stuffed leg of lamb, 86
Stuffed pork chops with
  pineapple-orange dressing,
  68
Stuffed tomatoes, baked, 92
Stuffing eleganté, 84
Sweet potatoes, marshmallow-
  date, 93
Sweet-sour sparerib bites, 161

Tarts
  for teas, serving suggestions,
    136
  lemon sunshine, 145

Tea
serving suggestions, 133-134, 145, 148, 150-152
varieties of, 151
Tea drops, chocolate orange, 146
Tetrazzini, turkey and ham, 113
Tomato and cucumber soup, chilled, 63
Tomato juice, serving suggestions, 52
Tomatoes
baked stuffed, 92
serving suggestions, 157
Torte, chocolate meringue, 98
Turkey
and ham Tetrazzini, 113
serving suggestions (buffet style), 82, 83, 85
smoked, and eggs supreme, 156
stuffing for, 84

Veal
Chinese, 67
cooked on skewers, 162
Vegetables, *see also* under name of vegetables
outdoor cooking of, 163-164, 166
serving suggestions, 68-69, 102
Vichyssoise, 62

Washington cherry ham glaze, 86
Wheaties nougat bars, 115
White mountain icing, 119

Subject Index

Apparel, proper, for guests, 12, 16, 133, 167

"Bread and butter notes," 32, 171
Candles, use of, 122, 134
Carving, 56-57, 78, 82-83, 85
Centerpieces, 55, 69-70, 122, 157
Children, participation of, in adult parties, 14, 147
Demitasses, 75
Diet problems, handling, 16-17
Dish washing, 100, 169
Entertaining, after dinner, 106-108
Flowers, as gift for hostess, 29-30
Games, 41-43, 158
Gifts, hostess, 29-30, 171-172
Guests
apparel of, 12, 16, 133, 167
arrival of, 27, 30, 44, 110, 120, 132, 155, 167
delayed, 30, 110, 155
departure of, 31-32, 108, 121, 132, 149, 158, 167-168, 171
diet problems of, handling, 16-17
house, 167-172
introduction of, 27-29, 133, 147-149
receiving, 14, 27, 133, 147
selection of, 10-11
Hand-shaking, 29
Introductions, 27-29, 133, 147-149
Invitations, 15-26
acceptance of, 16, 23, 25, 26, 110, 150, 167
addressing, 18
by telephone, 16, 150
diet problems, 16-17
engraved, 22
extended by hostess, 18-19, 21
last-minute, 20

mentioning other guests in, 18
printed cards, use of, 22
refusal of, 17, 23-25
rules for, 15, 23
timing of, 20
to after-dinner parties, 108
to brunch, 155, 158
to children's parties, 23
to house parties, 167
to late suppers, 109
to lunch, 120-121
to pot luck dinners, 101-102
to tea, 132-133, 150, 152
written, 21-22
Music, 42-43
Seating arrangements
buffet dinners, 80-81
lunches, 122
small dinner parties, 54-55
teas, 151
Serving hints and suggestions
brunches, 154-157
buffet meals, 78, 85, 92
coffee, 73-77, 100
late suppers, 115
salad, 60
small parties, 54, 56-58, 60, 64
stag parties, 116
teas, 133-135, 147-148, 150-152
Shopping list, importance of, 13-14, 79
Side tables, use of, 54
Smoking, at table, 130
Table setting
for buffet meals, 79-80
for lunches, 121
for small dinner parties, 55
for teas, 133-135
Tea service, 133-134, 150
Teacarts, use of, 54, 150
Telephone, invitations by, 16, 150
Thank-you notes, 32